An Introduction to
GENERAL KNOWLEDGE

Stanley Prince

PACKARD PUBLISHING LIMITED
CHICHESTER

An Introduction to
GENERAL KNOWLEDGE

First published in 1993 and reprinted with revisions in 1994, 1995 and 1997. This new edition published in 2000 and revised in 2004 by Packard Publishing Limited, Forum House, Stirling Road, Chichester, West Sussex, P019 7DN.

The publisher would like to thank Leo Stevenson for permission to reproduce his painting *Pass* on the front cover. Leo Stevenson's work is represented by Folio, 10 Gate Street, Lincoln's Inn Fields, London, WC2A 3HP.

ISBN 1 85341 126 4 (paperback only)

A CIP cataloguing record of this book is available from the British Library.

Typeset by Dorwyn Ltd, Rowlands Castle, Hampshire.
Printed and bound in the United Kingdom by DPS Partnership Ltd, Burgess Hill, West Sussex.

CONTENTS

FOREWORD

The original inspiration for this book was the Schools Challenge Quiz, based on the bell and buzzer contests of Bamber Gascoigne's *University Challenge*, which ran for many years on ITV and enjoyed immense popularity. As stated elsewhere, my school team became actively and successfully involved in the Junior Section of the Schools Challenge Quiz, and as I scrutinized past papers of Starter and Bonus questions, I began to seek ways of helping my own pupils imbibe all this wonderful knowledge in a more systematic and logical manner. Thus I made notes on a variety of topics including famous dates and battles in history, geographical capitals and currencies, Greek mythology, airports, airlines, international car registrations, inventors and assassinations. Eventually, prompted by the Bonus questions in particular, I had covered not only the realms of history, geography and science, but also literature, music, art, architecture, religion, sport and many other topics of general interest. It is this vastly expanded version of my original concept which I place before you.

My original aim has not changed in the ensuing years. It is quite simply to introduce to schoolchildren and students, in particular, but also to adult readers of any age, a compendium of human knowledge covering a wide range of topics and subjects, in the hope that they will be stimulated into learning facts which are of general interest, and into researching, more deeply, areas which have a particular appeal. Whilst some topics are, of necessity, complete in themselves, other sections provide information which is by no means definitive or exhaustive, and may prompt the reader to investigate further.

In terms of the National Curriculum, fact-based learning is slowly but surely coming back into vogue. I therefore trust that the information contained in this book on subjects such as mathematics, science, history, geography, literature, Greek mythology and the Roman World, will aid hard-pressed teachers in their endeavours, whilst the sections on religion, music and art will help to prevent these so-called peripheral subjects from falling into sad neglect. In short, I hope this book will be a formal back-up to areas of knowledge disseminated in schools and colleges, will stimulate readers of all ages, and will have the advantage of being easily transportable, which is one claim that cannot be made by a multi-volume encyclopaedia.

To the best of my knowledge and research, the facts in this book are correct at the time of going to print. However, if a budding question master wishes to use this material as a basis for a General Knowledge Quiz, it is as well to remember that facts do not always remain static. Three examples will suffice: (1) A country may change its currency or even its capital; (2) Recent space-probes have discovered that Jupiter, Saturn, Uranus and Neptune certainly have more satellites than were previously known to exist; (3) In this day and age it is more than likely that a football team may change its ground or even be declared bankrupt! So be prepared to double check to avoid the wrath of a wronged quiz participant. If justice is to be done, the question master's decision should only be final when he is right!

Finally, I should like to acknowledge the encouragement I have received from my publisher, and from many friends, who have made well-meaning and often helpful suggestions regarding material to be included. I should like to thank, in particular, Sarah Willard for her sterling efforts in helping me redraft and update the 2004 edition of this book, as well as Kevin Ashman and Trevor Montague for verifying some of the more contentious details. Good luck and happy reading!

Stanley Prince
Hove, East Sussex

HISTORY

A Brief Chronicle of Significant Events

BC	
c. 5000	Earliest settlements in Sumer, later called Mesopotamia (now Iraq), and Egypt (Nile Valley).
c. 3500	Discovery of bronze/Sumerian civilization flourishing/ Cuneiform (wedge-shaped) writing in use.
c. 3100	First Egyptian Dynasty.
c. 2870	First settlements at Troy.
c. 2700	Beginning of construction of Egyptian Pyramids.
c. 2100-1600	Construction of Stonehenge.
c. 1230	Exodus from Egypt of Israelites led by Moses.
c. 776	First Olympic Games take place.
c. 753	Traditional date for foundation of Rome (509 BC – Rome becomes a Republic).
586	Nebuchadnezzar captures Jerusalem.
490	Battle of Marathon (Athenians defeat Persians).
483	Death of Buddha (his name means the Enlightened-One).
480	Battles of Thermopylae and Salamis.
399	Death of Socrates (condemned by Athenian elders to drink hemlock).
347	Death of Plato – philosopher who wrote *The Republic* and other Socratic dialogues.
336	Alexander becomes King following assassination of his father Philip II of Macedon.
323	Death of Alexander the Great in Babylon aged 32.
322	Death of Aristotle – philosopher and tutor to Alexander the Great.
264-241	First Punic War between Rome and Carthage.
218	Beginning of Second Punic War – Hannibal crosses the Alps using elephants.
216	Battle of Cannae – Hannibal annihilates powerful Roman army.
c. 215	Construction of Great Wall of China (about 1,450 miles long).
202	Battle of Zama – Hannibal defeated by Scipio Africanus.
146	Carthage destroyed by Romans at end of Third Punic War.
73	Slaves revolt led by Spartacus the gladiator in Southern Italy.

71	Spartacus is killed and revolt quelled.
60	First Triumvirate – Pompey, Caesar and Crassus.
58-51	Julius Caesar conquers Gaul.
55&54	Caesar undertakes two invasions of Britain.
49	Caesar crosses the Rubicon – thus declaring war on Pompey and the Senate.
44	15th March (Ides): Julius Caesar murdered by Brutus, Cassius and other conspirators at the Senate.
43	Second Triumvirate – Mark Antony, Octavian and Lepidus.
42	Battle of Philippi – defeat and death of Brutus.
31	Battle of Actium – naval victory for Octavian over Antony and Cleopatra.
30	Antony commits suicide; Cleopatra kills herself with an asp.
27	Octavian declared first Roman Emperor by the Senate as Augustus Caesar.
c.4	Birth of Jesus Christ.
AD	
14	Death of Augustus Caesar.
c. 29	Crucifixion of Jesus Christ.
43	Roman Emperor Claudius (AD 41-54) invades Britain.
61	Revolt by Queen Boudicca (Boadicea) of the Iceni tribe against the Romans; she burns London and Colchester; later she poisons herself.
64	Great Fire of Rome/Deaths of St. Peter and St. Paul.
68	Roman Emperor Nero commits suicide – end of Julio-Claudian line of Roman Emperors.
70	Destruction of the Temple in Jerusalem.
79	Vesuvius erupts, destroying Pompeii, Herculaneum and Stabiae.
122-126	Construction of Hadrian's Wall (Tyne to the Solway).
142-200	Construction of Antonine Wall (Forth to the Clyde).
220	End of Han Dynasty in China.
306	Constantine proclaimed Emperor in York.
330	Constantinople (Byzantium) becomes new capital of Roman Empire.
410	Sack of Rome under Alaric the Visigoth.
435	Britain invaded by Angles, Saxons and Jutes.
451	Attila the Hun invades Gaul, but is defeated by Romans and Goths at Châlons.

c. 515	Battle of Mount Badon – Saxons defeated by Britons (possibly led by Arthur of legendary fame).
563	St. Columba founds mission in Iona.
570	Birth of the prophet Mohammed.
597	St. Augustine lands in Kent (602 – founds Canterbury Cathedral and becomes first Archbishop of Canterbury).
622	Hejira – Mohammed flees from Mecca to Medina (Islamic calendar dates from this event).
632	Death of Mohammed.
664	Synod of Whitby (ecclesiastical council which established the date of Easter and affirmed its support of the Roman Church).
778	Battle of Roncesvalles – defeat and death of Roland, famous warrior-knight.
782-3	Construction of Offa's Dyke (earthwork barrier between the Severn and the Dee). Offa was King of Mercia.
793	First Viking raid on Britain.
800	Christmas Day: Charlemagne crowned Holy Roman Emperor by Pope Leo III in Rome (this date is often considered the beginning of the Middle Ages).
828	Egbert, King of Wessex, acknowledged as overlord of all England.
843	Treaty of Verdun – France and Germany become separate states/Kenneth MacAlpin becomes Scotland's first King (uniting Picts and Scots).
868	Earliest dated printed book in China (Buddhist scripture, the Diamond Sutra, found in 1900).
871-899	Reign of Alfred the Great.
929	Death of Wenceslas, Christian Duke of Bohemia.
982	Eric 'the Red' discovers and colonizes Greenland on behalf of the Norsemen.
1000	Leif Ericsson (son of Eric 'the Red') discovers North America.
1014	Battle of Clontarf – victory of Irish under Brian Boru over Vikings.
1016	Canute becomes King of England.
1040	Macbeth slays Duncan.
1066	Battle of Stamford Bridge (Harold Godwinson defeats and kills Harald Hardrada and Tostig)/14th October: Battle of Hastings (Senlac Hill)/Christmas Day: William the Conqueror crowned King in Westminster Abbey.

1086	Domesday Book completed.
1170	Murder of Thomas à Becket in Canterbury Cathedral.
1215	15th June: King John sets his seal to the Magna Carta at Runnymede.
1264	Battle of Lewes (Henry III defeated by barons under Simon de Montfort).
1265	Simon de Montfort's Parliament/Battle of Evesham (defeat and death of de Montfort).
1314	24th June: Battle of Bannockburn – Robert Bruce defeats the English.
1346	Battle of Crécy (Black Prince wins his spurs).
1348	Black Death reaches Europe (1349 – England)/Order of the Garter established.
1356	Battle of Poitiers.
1368	Ming Dynasty in China (ends 1644).
1381	Peasants' Revolt (led by Wat Tyler).
1415	25th October: Battle of Agincourt (victory for Henry V).
1431	Burning of Joan of Arc at Rouen (canonized 1920).
1453	End of Hundred Years' War (1337-1453)/Constantinople captured by Turks.
1476	William Caxton sets up printing press (Westminster).
1485	Battle of Bosworth Field (Wars of the Roses 1455-85).
1488	Bartholomew Diaz rounds Cape of Good Hope.
1492	Christopher Columbus discovers West Indies.
1497	John Cabot discovers Newfoundland (first English colony).
1498	Vasco da Gama at Calicut; finds sea route to India.
1513	Battle of Flodden (James IV of Scotland killed).
1517	Martin Luther nails up 95 Theses (1521 – Diet of Worms).
1519	Ferdinand Magellan begins first circumnavigation of the world.
1520	Field of the Cloth of Gold (Henry VIII and Francis I).
1521	Hernándo Cortés conquers Mexico (Aztecs)/Magellan killed in Philippines.
1522	Sebastian del Cano completes first voyage around the world.
1525	Francis I captured at Pavia.
1532	Francisco Pizarro conquers Peru (Incas).
1533	Ivan IV (the Terrible) becomes first Russian Tsar.
1534	Act of Supremacy (Henry VIII head of English Church).
1536	Anne Boleyn executed/Thomas Cromwell dissolves monasteries.

1545	The *Mary Rose* sinks at Southsea.
1564	23rd April: Birth of Shakespeare (1616 – death of Shakespeare).
1571	Battle of Lepanto (Austrians defeat sea-power of Turks).
1577	Francis Drake navigates the globe (1580 – returns and is knighted aboard the *Golden Hind,* originally called the *Pelican*).
1587	Execution of Mary, Queen of Scots.
1588	Spanish Armada (Navy) defeated.
1603	James VI of Scotland unites English and Scottish crowns.
1605	5th November: Gunpowder Plot (Guy Fawkes fails in attempt to blow up the Houses of Parliament).
1610	Henry IV of France assassinated by François Ravaillac.
1611	King James Bible (authorized version of Bible).
1618	Defenestration of Prague begins Thirty Years' War.
1620	*Mayflower* – Pilgrim Fathers settle in New England.
1628	William Harvey publishes work on circulation of blood.
1642	English Civil War begins/Battle of Edgehill.
1644	Battle of Marston Moor.
1645	Battle of Naseby/New Model Army formed.
1649	30th January: Charles I executed (outside Banqueting House, Whitehall).
1651	Battle of Worcester – final defeat of Royalists.
1658	Death of Oliver Cromwell.
1660	Restoration of Monarchy under Charles II/Royal Society founded.
1665	Great Plague of London (approximately 69,000 deaths).
1666	Great Fire of London.
1678	'Popish Plot' of Titus Oates.
1685	Battle of Sedgemoor (Monmouth's rebellion crushed).
1688	The Glorious or Bloodless Revolution (William III and Mary II).
1690	Battle of the Boyne (James II defeated in Ireland).
1692	Massacre of Glencoe (Campbells massacre Macdonalds).
1694	Bank of England founded by Scotsman William Paterson.
1704	Capture of Gibraltar/Battle of Blenheim.
1706	Battle of Ramillies.
1707	Act of Union – English and Scottish Parliaments united.
1708	Battle of Oudenarde.
1709	Battle of Malplaquet.

1713	Treaty of Utrecht ends War of Spanish Succession.
1715	Defeat of James Edward Stuart (Old Pretender)/Death of Louis XIV (reigned 72 years – longest reign in European history).
1720	'South Sea Bubble'.
1721	Robert Walpole becomes first Prime Minister (1721-42).
1739	War of Jenkins' Ear.
1743	Battle of Dettingen (George II last British king to lead his army into battle).
1745	2nd Jacobite Rebellion – Charles Edward Stuart (Young Pretender) wins at Prestonpans – marches to Derby.
1746	16th April: Battle of Culloden Moor – 'Butcher' Cumberland defeats Bonnie Prince Charlie, saved by Flora Macdonald.
1752	Gregorian calendar introduced (3rd - 13th September omitted).
1756	Black Hole of Calcutta (only 23 survive out of 146).
1757	Battle of Plassey – victory for Clive of India.
1759	Battle of Quebec – Wolfe killed at Heights of Abraham.
1768	Royal Academy founded by Sir Joshua Reynolds.
1773	'Boston Tea Party' – American colonists throw chests of tea into Boston Harbour in protest over tea duty.
1775	American War of Independence/Battles of Lexington and Concord.
1776	4th July: American Declaration of Independence.
1777	Battle of Saratoga.
1781	General Cornwallis surrenders at Yorktown, Virginia.
1783	Treaty of Versailles/Montgolfier Brothers' hot air balloon/ William Pitt the Younger becomes Prime Minister at 24.
1789	George Washington becomes first President of USA/14th July: Storming of Bastille begins French Revolution.
1793	Executions of Louis XVI (January) and Marie Antoinette (October).
1798	Battle of the Nile (Aboukir Bay).
1801	lst January: Union of Great Britain and Ireland/First UK census/Battle of Copenhagen.
1804	Napoleon crowns himself Emperor of France in Notre Dame Cathedral in the presence of Pope Pius VII.
1805	21st October: Battle of Trafalgar (off Cape Trafalgar, a low headland in SW Spain) – Nelson killed on HMS *Victory*/ Battle of Austerlitz (The Three Emperors).
1807	Slave trade abolished in British Empire (1833 – slavery abolished).

1812	Retreat from Moscow – destruction of Napoleon's Grand Army.
1814	Abdication of Napoleon; Congress of Vienna (Napoleon exiled to Elba).
1815	18th June: Battle of Waterloo (12 miles from Brussels, Belgium)/Napoleon exiled to St Helena.
1819	Singapore founded by Sir Stamford Raffles.
1820	Death of George III (reigned for 60 years)/Cato Street conspiracy to assassinate British Cabinet.
1825	First railway opened – Stockton to Darlington.
1829	Rainhill Trials won by George Stephenson's Rocket/ Catholic Emancipation/Metropolitan Police Force established by Robert Peel/Greece becomes independent.
1834	'Tolpuddle Martyrs' deported to Australia for seven years.
1836	Great Trek of Boers/Texas becomes independent of Mexico (The Alamo).
1840	Penny Postage instituted by (Sir) Rowland Hill/Formal beginning of Opium War against China declared.
1842	Hong Kong (Fragrant Harbour) ceded to Britain by Treaty of Nanking.
1848	Year of Revolutions/*Communist Manifesto* by Marx and Engels/John Sutter discovers gold in California.
1851	Great Exhibition in Hyde Park – Crystal Palace.
1854	25th October: Charge of the Light Brigade at Balaclava during Crimean War.
1857	Indian Mutiny – Relief of Lucknow.
1859	Charles Darwin publishes *The Origin of Species*/Battle of Solferino (prompts Jean Henri Dunant to found Red Cross – 1864).
1861	American Civil War begins – Bull Run.
1863	Battle of Gettysburg.
1865	14th April: Assassination of Abraham Lincoln (Ford's Theatre, Washington)/Thirteenth Amendment to American Constitution confirms abolition of slavery in the USA.
1866	Seven Weeks' War (between Austria and Prussia).
1867	Dominion of Canada established/USA buys Alaska from Russia for $7,200,000 (Seward's Folly).
1869	Suez Canal opened; designed by Ferdinand de Lesseps.
1871	Henry Morton Stanley finds David Livingstone at Ujiji.
1876	General George Custer killed at Little Big Horn/Queen Victoria declared Empress of India by Parliament.

1879	Zulu War – Rorke's Drift/Tay Bridge disaster.
1885	General Charles Gordon killed at Khartoum.
1886	Daimler produces his first car.
1896	Gold discovered in the Klondike (Gold Rush – 1897).
1898	Battle of Omdurman/The Curies discover Radium.
1899	(Second) Boer War begins in South Africa.
1900	Battle of Spion Kop/Relief of Ladysmith and Mafeking/ Boxer Rebellion in China.
1901	22nd January: Queen Victoria dies (reigned 1837-1901).
1903	17th December: Wright brothers make first flight at Kill Devil Hill near Kitty Hawk, North Carolina.
1906	18th April: San Francisco earthquake.
1909	Robert Peary reaches North Pole/25th July: Louis Blériot makes first cross-channel flight.
1911	14th December: Roald Amundsen reaches South Pole.
1912	China becomes Republic under Sun Yat Sen/14th-15th April:*Titanic* sinks.
1914	Franz Ferdinand assassinated at Sarajevo/World War I begins.
1915	7th May: Sinking of *Lusitania.*
1916	Battles of Verdun, Jutland and the Somme.
1917	Vimy Ridge captured by Canadians/Russian Revolution by Bolsheviks.
1918	Women over 30 years old get the vote/11th November: Armistice Day.
1919	Alcock and Brown make first direct flight across the Atlantic.
1920	Prohibition in USA (ends 1933).
1921	Irish Free State set up/10th June: Birth of Prince Philip.
1924	Death of Lenin/First Labour Government under Ramsay MacDonald.
1926	General Strike in Britain (9 days)/21st April: Birth of Princess Elizabeth (future Queen Elizabeth II).
1927	Charles Lindbergh flies Atlantic solo in *Spirit of St. Louis,* New York-Paris.
1928	Women over 21 years old get the vote.
1929	St. Valentine's Day Massacre in Chicago/24th October: Wall Street Crash.
1930	R101 crashes at Beauvais/21st August: Birth of Princess Margaret.
1933	Hitler appointed Chancellor.

1934	Hitler becomes Dictator (Führer).
1935	Mussolini invades Abyssinia.
1936	Civil War begins in Spain (until 1939)/Jarrow Hunger March to London/Abdication of Edward VIII.
1938	29th September: Munich Peace Pact.
1939	Mussolini invades Albania/lst September: Germany invades Poland/3rd September: World War II begins/Battle of River Plate – *Graf Spee* scuttled in Montevideo harbour.
1940	Dunkirk evacuated (May-June)/Battle of Britain (September)/Leon Trotsky assassinated in Mexico.
1941	HMS *Hood* sunk/*Bismarck* sunk/HMS *Ark Royal* sunk/7th December: Japanese bomb Pearl Harbour (Hawaii)/Hong Kong surrenders (Christmas Day).
1942	15th February: Singapore surrenders/Malta awarded George Cross/1,000 bomber raid on Cologne.
1943	Italy surrenders.
1944	6th June: D-Day Landings by Allies/25th August: Paris liberated/Battle for Arnhem.
1945	Yalta Conference/Dresden bombed/Mussolini shot by partisans/Hitler commits suicide in Berlin bunker/8th May: World War II ends in Europe/Atomic bombs dropped on Hiroshima (6th August) and Nagasaki (9th August)/Japan surrenders (14th August).
1946	United Nations established in New York under Norwegian Trygve Lie, first UN Secretary-General.
1947	lst January: Coal Industry nationalized/Chuck Yeager breaks sound barrier/India partitioned.
1948	lst January: British Railways nationalized/30th January: Mahatma Gandhi assassinated in New Delhi/14th May: Israel proclaimed a State/14th November: Birth of Prince Charles.
1949	lst May: Gas Industry nationalized.
1950	Korean War begins/15th August: Birth of Princess Anne.
1951	Festival of Britain takes place.
1952	6th February: Elizabeth II ascends throne/USA tests hydrogen bomb.
1953	Death of Stalin/29th May: Colonel John Hunt's Everest expedition; Edmund Hillary and Sherpa Norgay Tenzing reach summit/2nd June: Coronation of Queen Elizabeth II.
1954	6th May: Roger Bannister breaks the 4-minute mile at Iffley Road track, Oxford/Food rationing ends in Britain.

1955	Death of Albert Einstein/Ruth Ellis (last woman) hanged.
1956	Suez crisis/Hungarian uprising/First atomic power station at Calder Hall/3rd class rail travel abolished.
1957	EEC and Euratom treaties signed/4th October: Russians launch *Sputnik I*/3rd November: *Sputnik II* – first dog in space ('Laika').
1958	lst January: EEC treaty comes into force.
1959	Fidel Castro overthrows Batista in Cuba/Christopher Cockerell's prototype hovercraft, the SR.N1, makes the Calais–Dover crossing of the English Channel.
1960	First working laser/19th February: Birth of Prince Andrew.
1961	12th April: Yuri Gagarin first man in space/5th May: Al Shepard first American in space/Building of the Berlin Wall.
1962	February: John Glenn first American to orbit the Earth/ Algeria achieves independence from France/Launch of Telstar communications satellite.
1963	Valentina Tereshkova first woman in space in *Vostok 6*/ 22nd November: John F. Kennedy assassinated.
1964	10th March: Birth of Prince Edward/Opening of BBC2/ Last man hanged in UK.
1965	Winston Churchill dies/Alexei Leonov makes first space walk/Unilateral Declaration of Independence (UDI) declared by Ian Smith in Rhodesia/Abolition of death penalty for murder in UK.
1966	Assassination of Dr Verwoerd (South Africa)/England beat West Germany 4 – 2 in the World Cup Final/Aberfan disaster (144 killed).
1967	June: Six Day War between Israel and Arabs/Christiaan Barnard performs first heart transplant on Louis Washkansky.
1968	Assassinations of Martin Luther King and Bobby Kennedy/ Invasion of Czechoslovakia by Soviet Union.
1969	lst July: Investiture of Prince of Wales/21st July: Neil Armstrong walks on the Moon (NB. 20th July in USA).
1970	Deaths of President Nasser (Egypt) and Charles de Gaulle (France).
1971	15th February: Decimalization of currency.

1972 Idi Amin expels Ugandan Asians.

1973 lst January: Britain, Ireland and Denmark join the Common Market/lst April: VAT introduced in Britain/ 'Watergate' scandal in USA/October: Yom Kippur War/14th November: Wedding of Princess Anne and Captain Mark Phillips in Westminster Abbey.

1974 Richard M. Nixon resigns as President of USA/Miners' Strike in Britain.

1975 Death of General Franco/EEC Referendum in UK.

1976 Deaths of Chou En-Lai (Prime Minister) and Mao Tse-Tung (Chairman) of People's Republic of China/Concorde enters supersonic passenger service/Israeli raid on Entebbe airport.

1977 Queen's Silver Jubilee/16th August: Death of Elvis Presley/14th October: Death of Bing Crosby.

1978 First test-tube baby (Louise Brown).

1979 Islamic Revolution in Iran/Soviet invasion of Afghanistan.

1980 Zimbabwe achieves independence/December: John Lennon murdered by Mark David Chapman in New York.

1981 29th July: Royal Wedding of Prince Charles and Lady Diana Spencer in St. Paul's Cathedral.

1982 Falklands War begins/2lst June: Birth of Prince William.

1983 Sally Ride becomes first American woman in space.

1984 Soviet cosmonaut becomes first woman to walk in space/ 15th September: Birth of Prince Henry/12th October: IRA bomb explosion at Grand Hotel, Brighton/Indira Gandhi assassinated by Sikhs.

1985 Border between Spain and Gibraltar reopened/Fire at Bradford City FC/38 killed during soccer violence at Heysel Stadium (Brussels) before Liverpool v. Juventus European Cup Final/Two explosions sink Greenpeace campaign ship *Rainbow Warrior*.

1986 *Challenger* shuttle crashes after take off – all seven on board killed/Olof Palme, Swedish Prime Minister, assassinated/First issue of *Today* newspaper published (March)/28th April: Nuclear power accident at Chernobyl/23rd July: Royal Wedding of Prince Andrew and Sarah Ferguson in Westminster Abbey/First issue of *The Independent* newspaper published (October).

1987 Terry Waite, Archbishop of Canterbury's special envoy, disappears in Beirut/Townsend Thoresen ferry, *Herald of Free Enterprise,* capsizes outside Zeebrugge/Princess Anne given the title of Princess Royal/Fiji declared a Republic/ Suicide of Rudolf Hess in Spandau Prison/16th October: 19 killed and trees and property devastated by hurricane in southern Britain/19th October: Black Monday with Stock Exchange crash of shares in London and New York/ Remembrance Day bomb at Enniskillen/Escalator fire at King's Cross station.

1988 Liberals and SDP form the Social and Liberal Democratic Party; Paddy Ashdown elected leader of SLDP/8th August: Birth of Princess Beatrice/President Zia of Pakistan killed as aircraft explodes/Clapham railcrash (2 trains collide)/ Pan Am jumbo jet crashes on Lockerbie.

1989 Death of Emperor Hirohito of Japan/Boeing 737 crashes on Ml motorway near Kegworth, Leicestershire/Launch of Sky television/Salman Rushdie goes into hiding after Ayatollah Khomeini orders his execution for blasphemy over *The Satanic Verses*/95 Liverpool supporters crushed to death at Hillsborough, Sheffield/2nd June: Hundreds of Chinese students massacred in Tiananmen Square/Death of Ayatollah Khomeini/Death of Lord Olivier/Guildford Four released from jail/First TV Broadcast from House of Commons/Revolution in Eastern Europe: Poland – Solidarity gains victory in elections/Hungary – 6,000 East German refugees are allowed to escape to the West; New Hungarian Republic proclaimed/East Germany – opens all borders to the West and dismantles the Berlin Wall/Czechoslovakia – opens borders to the West; Communist rule ends; Václav Havel becomes President/ Romania – bloodshed in Bucharest and Timisoara eventually leads to arrest and execution of Nicolae and Elena Ceausescu.

1990 Scientists find evidence of global warming/Hurricane-force winds buffet southern England – 46 die, 3 million trees destroyed/F.W. de Klerk lifts ban on ANC/Nelson Mandela freed from jail after 25 years/23rd March: Birth of Princess Eugenie/Anti Poll Tax demonstration in London ends in violence and looting/Iraq invades Kuwait on the orders of President Saddam Hussein/Reunification of Germany with

Berlin as the capital in name only/22nd November: Margaret Thatcher resigns as Prime Minister after 11½ years in office.

1991 Gulf War in Middle East lasts 6 weeks, ending on 27th February after Kuwait is liberated by Allies – Mission codenamed Operation Desert Storm/IRA bomb attack on 10 Downing Street/Birmingham Six freed after 16 years in jail/Sanctions against South Africa are lifted and world sporting ties resumed as country moves towards dismantling apartheid laws/Helen Sharman becomes first British astronaut/21st May: Rajiv Gandhi assassinated by female suicide bomber (subsequent investigations suggest her name was Thanu)/Serbia and Croatia fight Civil War in Yugoslavia/Hostages John McCarthy (August) and Terry Waite (November) released from 5 years captivity in Beirut/Maastricht Summit on European Unity/USSR – 19th August: Gorbachev toppled by coup; 21st August: Gorbachev restored as President after resistance led by Boris Yeltsin/Communist rule ends/Baltic states recognized as independent/Soviet Union is ended/25th December: Gorbachev resigns as President.

1992 Boutros Boutros-Ghali appointed as new UN Secretary-General/Georgia is recognized as independent/Yugoslavia – European Community recognizes Croatia and Slovenia as independent republics; Bulgaria also recognizes independence of Macedonia; war rages in Bosnia-Herzegovina with fierce fighting between Serbs and Muslims as Serbian troops devastate Sarajevo/Ireland – Charles Haughey resigns and is succeeded by Albert Reynolds/Algeria – state of emergency declared after riots by Muslim fundamentalists/South Africa – rioting and violence in townships/John Major wins record-breaking 4th term of office for Conservative party in General Election/Euro-Disney opens near Paris/Betty Boothroyd appointed first ever woman Speaker of House of Commons/20th November: Fire causes severe damage to St. George's Hall and other parts of Windsor Castle/10th December: Formal separation of the Prince and Princess of Wales announced/12th December: Second marriage of Princess Anne, to Cdr Timothy Laurence, at Crathie Church near Balmoral, Scotland/31st December: Czechoslovakia divided into Czech Republic and Slovakia at midnight.

1993 1st January: Single European market comes into force/Liberian-registered oil tanker *Braer* runs aground at Garths Ness, South Shetland causing widespread pollution/Death of ballet dancer Rudolf Nureyev/Terrorist bomb explosion under Manhattan's World Trade Centre kills 7 and injures 1,000/IRA bombs at Warrington and Bishopsgate, City of London/Huge opposition to government proposals to privatize railways and impose VAT on domestic fuel/Grand National declared void/Siege in Waco, Texas ends as cult members commit mass suicide/7th August: Buckingham Palace opens to the public to fund Windsor Castle repairs/World's number 1 tennis player Monica Seles stabbed by spectator in Germany/Bomb damages Uffizi Gallery, Florence/Britain ratifies Maastricht Treaty despite parliamentary setbacks over Social Chapter/13th September: Yitzhak Rabin of Israel and Yasser Arafat of the PLO sign historic agreement in Washington promising Palestinian limited self-rule in exchange for recognition of Israel's right to peaceful existence/13th December: Vladimir Zhirinovsky's Nationalist Party wins majority of seats in Russian Parliament/22nd December: Formal ending of *apartheid* in South Africa/31st December: European Monetary Institute established in Frankfurt at midnight.

1994 January: Severe floods in England – Chichester inundated/IRA mortar attacks on Heathrow airport/First women Anglican priests ordained/Nelson Mandela becomes President of South Africa following first democratic elections/Ayrton Senna killed at Imola/Civil war in Rwanda involving mass genocide/6th May: Official opening of Channel Tunnel/Labour Party leader John Smith dies and is succeeded by Tony Blair/50th anniversary of D-Day commemorated/IRA (31st August) and Loyalists (13th October) declare ceasefires leading to talks between British Government and Gerry Adams of Sinn Fein/World's oldest human fossils found in Ethiopia/*Estonia* ferry disaster in the Baltic claims 910 lives/Israel and Jordan sign peace treaty/19th November: First National Lottery draw in Britain/Ireland – Albert Reynolds resigns and is replaced by John Bruton/Russia invades breakaway republic of Chechnya, shelling its capital Grozny/31st December: 4-month truce declared in Bosnia/Austria, Finland and Sweden join EU at midnight.

1995 January: Earthquake devastates Kobe, Japan/Nick Leeson loses £860 million causing collapse of Barings, Britain's oldest merchant bank/Alison Hargreaves climbs Everest solo and without oxygen, but dies climbing K2/Lisa Clayton becomes first woman to sail solo around the world/50th anniversaries of VE and VJ days commemorated/Warfare resumes in Bosnia (May) – peace agreed (October) – treaty signed in Paris (December)/*Today* newspaper closes/ Deaths of former PMs Lord Home and Lord Wilson/O.J. Simpson found not guilty of two murders in Los Angeles/ 4th November: Yitzhak Rabin, Israeli Prime Minister, assassinated in Tel Aviv/Prince William goes to Eton/ Princess Diana's *Panorama* interview sparks Queen's request for royal divorce.

1996 Death of former French President François Mitterand/ Death of Gene Kelly/9th February: IRA bomb damages Canary Wharf in the London Docklands/200 injured in IRA bomb outrage in Manchester/Oil tanker *Sea Empress* runs aground off Wales causing environmental disaster/Prince and Princess of Wales divorce/Death of comedian George Burns aged 100/Duke and Duchess of York divorce/ Headmaster Philip Lawrence murdered outside his school/ Fire closes Channel Tunnel for two weeks/Rower, Steve Redgrave, wins record equalling 4th Olympic gold medal/Damon Hill becomes Formula One Motor Racing World Champion/Stone of Scone is returned to Scotland after 700 years.

1997 O.J. Simpson ordered to pay £15 million pounds after being found guilty in civil court/Death of Chinese Premier Deng Xiaoping aged 92/Bridgewater Three freed after 18 years in jail/Dolly the Sheep cloned by scientists/30th March: Opening of Channel 5/Grand National on a Monday following a bomb hoax/lst May: Landslide victory for Labour Party in General Election (419 seats – overall majority 179)/Chess computer Deep Blue defeats Gary Kasparov/Zaire renamed Democratic Republic of Congo/ William Hague becomes youngest Tory leader since 1783/Hong Kong handed over to Chinese/Deaths of

Jacques Cousteau, Robert Mitchum and James Stewart/Slobodan Milosevic becomes President of Yugoslavia/31st August: Diana, Princess of Wales, killed in car crash in Paris along with Dodi Fayed/6th September: Funeral of Diana at Westminster Abbey/Death of Mother Teresa of Calcutta/Referenda in favour of Scottish Parliament and Welsh Assembly/Fiji readmitted to Commonwealth/John Denver killed in plane crash/*Thrust* breaks sound barrier on land/BBC begins 24-hour news channel/Windsor Castle reopened/Queen celebrates golden wedding anniversary.

1998 President Clinton denies relationship with Monica Lewinsky/Deaths of Enoch Powell and Dr Benjamin Spock/*Titanic* wins 11 Oscars to equal *Ben Hur*/10th April: Good Friday peace agreement in Northern Ireland/Deaths of Tammy Wynette and Linda McCartney/Official launch of Euro at Brussels Summit/Death of Frank Sinatra/Arsenal win League and Cup double/Serbian massacres of ethnic Albanians in Kosovo/David Trimble elected First Minister of N.I./France wins World Cup/Bomb in Omagh, County Tyrone kills 28/Frenchman Benoit Lecomte first to swim the Atlantic/MCC votes to admit women members; Channel 4 acquires rights to show Test Matches/Deaths of Poet Laureate Ted Hughes and wrestler Giant Haystacks/John Hume and David Trimble receive Nobel peace prize/Anglo-American air strikes against Iraq with bombing of Baghdad/President Clinton impeached on 2 counts.

1999 Glenn Hoddle sacked as England manager after reincarnation interview/Death of King Hussein of Jordan aged 63/Row over genetically modified foods/Clinton acquitted by Senate on charges of perjury and obstruction of justice/Deaths of violinist Yehudi Menuhin and comedian Ernie Wise/Successful round-the-world balloon trip ends after 20 days/NATO forces bomb Belgrade as ethnic cleansing of Albanians escalates in Kosovo/Nail bombs in London's Brixton, Brick Lane and Soho/Murder of TV presenter Jill Dando/Manchester Utd. achieve League, F.A. Cup and European Cup treble/19th June: Royal Wedding of Prince Edward and Sophie Rhys-Jones in St. George's Chapel, Windsor; royal couple created Earl and Countess of Wessex/Final Royal Tournament at Earl's

Court/Charles Kennedy becomes leader of Liberal Democrats/11th August: First total eclipse seen in mainland Britain since 1927/Scottish Parliament and Welsh Assembly set up/N.I. Assembly with power-sharing executive established at Stormont/31 die in Paddington rail disaster/End of hereditary peers in the House of Lords (92 survive)/Lennox Lewis becomes undisputed World Heavyweight Boxing Champion/30th December: former Beatle George Harrison stabbed by intruder/31st December: Boris Yeltsin resigns as Russian President/The Queen inaugurates Millennium Dome at North Greenwich at 11 p.m. GMT.

2000 Dr Harold Shipman convicted of murdering 15 elderly women patients in Greater Manchester/1st February: The London Eye officially opens to the public/Pierre-Yves Gerbeau replaces Jennie Page as Chief Executive of the Millennium Dome/Austria elects extreme right-wing administration/Labour Party celebrates centenary of its foundation/Death of Sir Stanley Matthews aged 85/Tate Gallery renamed Tate Britain/Vladimir Putin sworn in as Russian President/Ken Livingstone elected London's Mayor/Queen opens Millennium Bridge (9th May) and Tate Modern (11th May) – bridge closed down due to 'wobble' (12th June)/Cherie Blair gives birth to Leo/Death of President Assad of Syria/113 die when Air France Concorde crashes into a hotel minutes after leaving Charles de Gaulle airport/ 86 convicted terrorists released from Maze prison in N.I. under Good Friday Agreement/4th August: Queen Mother celebrates 100th birthday/Deaths of actor Sir Alec Guinness and broadcaster Sir Robin Day/England beat the West Indies in 4th Test at Headingley in under 2 days/118 crew perish when the Russian nuclear submarine *Kursk* sinks in the Barents Sea/Missile attack on MI6 headquarters/ Kevin Keegan resigns as England soccer coach following 1-0 defeat by Germany in last match staged at Wembley/Death of First Minister for Scotland, Donald Dewar/Hatfield rail disaster kills 4 and injures 35/Enigma coding machine, stolen from Bletchley Park Museum, posted to Jeremy Paxman/Judith Keppel becomes first contestant to win £1million on *Who Wants To Be A Millionaire?*/Netherlands first country to legalise euthanasia/13th December: Al Gore finally concedes defeat in US Presidential Election race/31st December: Millennium Dome Experience closes to public at 6 p.m.

2001 George W(alker) Bush becomes 43rd President of USA/Massive earthquake hits India/Ariel Sharon elected Prime Minister of Israel/Outbreak of foot and mouth disease forces mass slaughter of British livestock/GNER Express and goods train collide after Land Rover plummets off M62 near Selby, North Yorkshire/IRA bomb explodes outside BBC TV Centre/Death of Australian cricketing legend Donald Bradman aged 92/Russian space station *Mir* splashes down in Pacific Ocean after 15 years in orbit/Slobodan Milosevic arrested in Yugoslavia/Train robber Ronnie Biggs returns to Britain from Brazil/Dennis Tito becomes first space tourist/Death of writer Douglas Adams aged 49/Liverpool win Worthington Cup, FA Cup and UEFA Cup treble/Old Etonian, Crown Prince Dipendra, massacres members of his Nepalese Royal Family/Jeffrey Archer sentenced to 4 years' imprisonment/ IRA bomb injures 11 in Ealing/11th September: Terrorists crash 2 hijacked planes into World Trade Centre destroying Twin Towers and killing 3,000 victims; a third plane hits the Pentagon and a fourth crashes in Pennsylvania/ USA, supported by Britain, bombs Afghanistan after Osama bin Laden is held responsible for terrorist outrage of 11th September/5 die after anthrax spores are posted in USA/ Death of Britain's first Chess Grand Master, Tony Miles, aged 46/29th November: Death of George Harrison in Los Angeles aged 58/NZ yachting hero Sir Peter Blake shot dead by pirates in Brazil/Leaning Tower of Pisa reopens after almost 12 years/USA captures Tora Bora caves, last *al Qaeda* stronghold in eastern Afghanistan.

2002 1st January: 12 EU countries officially adopt the Euro/*Starlight Express* closes after 18 years/9th February: Death of Princess Margaret aged 71/Millennium Bridge reopens to the public/Cricketer Ben Hollioake killed in car crash aged 24/Halle Berry becomes first black woman to win Best Actress Oscar/Death of Dudley Moore aged 66/30th March: Death of Queen Mother aged 101/ Following a spate of suicide bomb outrages, Israel declares a state of war and invades a number of Palestinian towns on the West Bank/Colin Powell visits Middle East on a peace mission/Arsenal win League and Cup double for the third time/Train derailment at Potters Bar, Hertfordshire kills 7/*Cats*, the West End's longest running musical, closes on its 21st birthday/Patricia Amos becomes Britain's first person jailed for failing to send her children to school/3rd June: Queen celebrates Golden Jubilee with garden party in grounds of Buckingham Palace culminating in a pop concert and firework display/Lennox Lewis knocks out Mike Tyson to retain World Heavyweight title/Brazil wins World Cup for record fifth time/Michael Schumacher wins record 11 Formula One Grand Prix races in a season/ Hundreds killed and injured by bomb explosions on Bali, Indonesia/Paula Radcliffe breaks women's world marathon record by 89 seconds in Chicago/UN inspectors search Iraq for evidence concerning weapons of mass destruction.

2003 Death of Maurice Gibb/1st February: *Columbia* space shuttle breaks up on re-entry/Worldwide anti-war protests held/Yugoslavia renamed Serbia and Montenegro/Deaths of Adam Faith and Barry Sheene/SARS virus epidemic/19th March: Invasion of Iraq begins/9th April: Fall of Baghdad/ Major Charles Ingram convicted of cheating on *Who Wants To Be A Millionaire?*/1st May: Bush declares combat in Iraq and Afghanistan over/Baroness Amos becomes first black woman in British Cabinet/Deaths of Gregory Peck, Barry White and Bob Hope aged 100/Dr David Kelly commits suicide leading to Hutton inquiry/Largest ever power failure hits North America/Anna Lindh, Swedish foreign minister, assassinated/Sweden votes no to joining Euro/ Death of Johnny Cash/David Blaine ends 44-day stunt in glass box over Thames/Michael Howard becomes new leader of Conservative Party/22nd November: England win Rugby World Cup beating Australia 20pts–17pts in the final/Zimbabwe quits Commonwealth/Capture of Saddam Hussein/Libya agrees to scrap weapons of mass destruction programmes/Earthquake devastates Bam, Iran/Deaths of Sir Alan Bates and Bob Monkhouse.

Kings and Queens of England

Important Saxons		
Egbert		828-39
Ethelbert		860-66
Alfred the Great		871-99
Athelstan		925-40
Edgar	(The Peaceful)	959-75
Edward	(The Martyr)	975-78
Ethelred II	(The Unready)	978-1016
Edmund Ironside		1016
Danes		
Canute (Knut)		1016-35
Harold I	(Harold Harefoot)	1035-40
Hardicanute		1040-42
Saxons		
Edward the Confessor		1042-66
Harold II	(Harold Godwinson)	1066
Normans		
William I	(The Conqueror)	1066-87
William II	(Rufus)	1087-1100
Henry I	(The Lion of Justice), (Beauclerc)	1100-35
Stephen		1135-54
Plantagenets		
Henry II	(Curtmantle), (The Lawyer King)	1154-89
Richard I	(Coeur de Lion), (The Lionheart)	1189-99
John	(Lackland)	1199-1216
Henry III	(The Builder)	1216-72
Edward I	(The Hammer of the Scots), (Longshanks)	1272-1307
Edward II	(Edward of Caernarvon)	1307-27
Edward III		1327-77
Richard II	(Richard of Bordeaux)	1377-99

House of Lancaster

Henry IV	(Henry Bolingbroke)	1399-1413
Henry V	(Henry of Monmouth)	1413-22
Henry VI		1422-61; 1470-71

House of York

Edward IV	(The Rose of Rouen)	1461-70; 1471-83
Edward V		1483
Richard III	(Crookback)	1483-85

House of Tudor

Henry VII		1485-1509
Henry VIII	(Bluff King Hal)	1509-47
Edward VI		1547-53
Jane	(The Nine-Day Queen)	1553 (9 days)
Mary I	(Bloody Mary)	1553-58
Elizabeth I	(Good Queen Bess), (The Virgin Queen)	1558-1603

Kings and Queens of Britain

House of Stuart

James I	(The Wisest Fool in Christendom)	1603-25
Charles I	(Charles, King and Martyr)	1625-49

Commonwealth (Lord Protectors)

Oliver Cromwell	(Old Noll)	1653-58
Richard Cromwell	(Tumbledown Dick)	1658-59

House of Stuart (Restoration)

Charles II	(Old Rowley), (The Merry Monarch)	1660-85
James II		1685-88
William III of Orange }		1689-1702
and Mary II }		1689-94
Anne	(Brandy Nan)	1702-14

House of Hanover

George I		1714-27
George II		1727-60

George III	(Farmer George)	1760-1820
George IV	(The First Gentleman of Europe), (Prinny)	1820-30
William IV	(The Sailor King), (Silly Billy)	1830-37
Victoria	(The Widow of Windsor)	1837-1901

House of Saxe-Coburg Gotha (1901-1917)

Edward VII	(The Peace-Maker)	1901-10

House of Windsor (from 1917)

George V		1910-36
Edward VIII	(The People's King)	1936 (325 days)
George VI		1936-52
Elizabeth II		1952-

Important Kings and Queens of Scotland

House of Alpin

Kenneth MacAlpin		843-60
Malcolm II		1005-34

House of Atholl

Duncan I		1034-40
Macbeth		1040-57
Malcolm III Canmore	(Large Head)	1058-93
Alexander I	(The Fierce)	1107-24
David I	(The Saint)	1124-53
Malcolm IV	(The Maiden)	1153-65
William I	(The Lion)	1165-1214
Alexander II		1214-49
Alexander III		1249-86
Margaret	(The Maid of Norway)	1286-90

House of Balliol

John (Balliol)		1292-96

House of Bruce

Robert I (Bruce)		1306-29
David II		1329-71

House of Stewart

Robert II	1371-90
Robert III	1390-1406
James I	1406-37
James II	1437-60
James III	1460-88
James IV	1488-1513
James V	1513-42
Mary, Queen of Scots	1542-67
James VI	1567-1625

(He became James I of England in 1603.)

Important Kings of Ireland

Brian Boru	1002-14

Ireland was divided into five kingdoms: Ulster, Munster, Leinster, Connaught and Meath, over all of which a High King reigned. Ireland's greatest king Brian Boru, King of Munster, was assassinated in his observation tent after the Battle of Clontarf in 1014, a great victory over the Danes. The supremacy of his descendants, the O'Briens, ended in 1119. Henry II invaded Ireland in 1171 and styled himself Lord of Ireland in 1177. In 1497 Henry VII took away the independence of the Irish Parliament by an Act known as Poynings' Law. By Act of Parliament in 1542 Henry VIII styled himself King of Ireland.

Important Sovereign Princes of Wales

Owain Gwynedd		1137-70
Dafydd I		1170-94
Llywelyn Fawr	(the Great)	1194-1240
Dafydd II		1240-46
Llywelyn ap Gruffydd	(the Last)	1246-82

Wales' most celebrated native prince was Llywelyn the Great. His son Gruffydd fell into English hands and was killed attempting to escape from the Tower of London. Edward I defeated Llywelyn ap Gruffydd, the last native Prince of Wales, and made his own son, Edward, Prince of Wales in 1301. Since then the reigning sovereign's eldest son has usually been created Prince of Wales.

Royal Homes

Occupied Royal Palaces

Buckingham Palace London
(Official English Royal Residence of the Monarch since 1837)
Windsor Castle Royal Berkshire
Holyroodhouse Palace Edinburgh
(Official Royal Residence of the Monarch when in Scotland)
Kensington Palace London
(London Residences of the Duke and Duchess of Gloucester, and Prince and Princess Michael of Kent)
Clarence House London
(London Residence of the Prince of Wales)
St James's Palace London
(London Residences of Princess Alexandra and the Hon. Sir Angus Ogilvy)

Historical (unoccupied) Royal Palaces

The Tower of London
Hampton Court
Kensington State Apartments
Banqueting House, Whitehall
Kew Palace

Other Royal Homes

Sandringham House Norfolk
Balmoral Castle Aberdeenshire
Osborne House Isle of Wight (English Heritage)
Highgrove House Gloucestershire
(Private country home of the Prince of Wales)
Gatcombe Park Gloucestershire
(Private country home of the Princess Royal)
Bagshot Park Surrey
(Private home of the Earl and Countess of Wessex)
Castle of Mey Caithness

Prime Ministers of Britain

1. Sir Robert Walpole	(Whig)	1721-42
2. Earl of Wilmington	(Whig)	1742-3
3. Henry Pelham	(Whig)	1743-54
4. Duke of Newcastle	(Whig)	1754-6; 1757-62

5. Duke of Devonshire	(Whig)	1756-7
6. Earl of Bute	(Tory)	1762-3
7. George Grenville	(Whig)	1763-5
8. Marquess of Rockingham	(Whig)	1765-6
9. William Pitt the Elder, Earl of Chatham (The Great Commoner)	(Whig)	1766-8
10. Duke of Grafton	(Whig)	1768-70
11. Lord North	(Tory)	1770-82
12. Earl of Shelburne	(Whig)	1782-3
13. Duke of Portland	(Tory)	1783; 1807-9
14. William Pitt the Younger	(Tory)	1783-1801; 1804-6
15. Henry Addington	(Tory)	1801-4
16. Lord Grenville	(Whig)	1806-7
17. Spencer Perceval	(Tory)	1809-12
18. Lord Liverpool	(Tory)	1812-27
19. George Canning	(Tory)	1827
20. Viscount Goderich	(Tory)	1827-8
21. Arthur Wellesley, Duke of Wellington	(Tory)	1828-30
22. Earl Grey	(Whig)	1830-4
23. Viscount Melbourne	(Whig)	1834; 1835-41
24. Sir Robert Peel	(Tory) (Conservative)	1834-5; 1841-6
25. Lord John Russell	(Whig)	1846-52; 1865-6
26. Earl of Derby	(Conservative)	1852; 1858-9; 1866-8
27. Earl of Aberdeen	(Tory or Peelite)	1852-5
28. Viscount Palmerston	(Liberal)	1855-8; 1859-65
29. Benjamin Disraeli (Earl of Beaconsfield)	(Conservative)	1868; 1874-80
30. William Ewart Gladstone	(Liberal)	1868-74; 1880-5; 1886; 1892-4
31. Marquess of Salisbury	(Conservative)	1885-6; 1886-92; 1895-1902
32. Earl of Rosebery	(Liberal)	1894-5
33. Arthur Balfour	(Conservative)	1902-5
34. Sir Henry Campbell-Bannerman	(Liberal)	1905-8
35. Herbert Henry Asquith	(Liberal)	1908-16
36. David Lloyd George	(Liberal)	1916-22
37. Andrew Bonar Law	(Conservative)	1922-3

38. Stanley Baldwin	(Conservative)	1923; 1924-9; 1935-7
39. (James) Ramsay MacDonald	(Labour)	1924; 1929-35
40. (Arthur) Neville Chamberlain	(Conservative)	1937-40
41. Sir Winston Churchill	(Conservative)	1940-5 (Coalition); 1951-5
42. Clement Attlee	(Labour)	1945-51
43. Sir Anthony Eden (Lord Avon)	(Conservative)	1955-7
44. (Maurice) Harold Macmillan (Supermac)	(Conservative)	1957-63
45. Sir Alec Douglas-Home	(Conservative)	1963-4
46. (James) Harold Wilson	(Labour)	1964-70; 1974-6
47. Edward Heath	(Conservative)	1970-4
48. (Leonard) James Callaghan (Gentleman Jim)	(Labour)	1976-9
49. Margaret Thatcher (The Iron Lady)	(Conservative)	1979-90
50. John Major	(Conservative)	1990-7
51. Tony Blair	(Labour)	1997-

Parliaments

UK	–	Parliament (House of Commons and House of Lords).
Isle of Man	–	Tynwald (lower house is The House of Keys).
Republic of Ireland (Eire)	–	Dáil (Eireann).
USA		Congress (House of Representatives and Senate).
France	–	Assemblée Nationale.
Germany	–	Bundestag and Bundesrat.
Netherlands	–	States-General.
Italy	–	Senato (Senate).
Spain	–	Cortes.
Portugal	–	Cortes.
Iceland	–	Althing (world's oldest Parliament).
Norway	–	Storting.
Denmark	–	Folketing.
Sweden	–	Riksdag.
Russia	–	Duma (lower chamber).
Israel	–	Knesset.
Japan	–	Diet.
India	–	Lok Sabha and Rajya Sabha.

Presidents of the United States

1. George Washington	(Federal)	1789-97
2. John Adams	(Federal)	1797-1801
3. Thomas Jefferson (The Sage of Monticello)	(Republican)	1801-09
4. James Madison (Father of the Constitution)	(Republican)	1809-17
5. James Monroe	(Republican)	1817-25
6. John Quincy Adams	(Republican)	1825-29
7. Andrew Jackson (Old Hickory)	(Democrat)	1829-37
8. Martin Van Buren (The Little Magician)	(Democrat)	1837-41
9. William Henry Harrison	(Whig)	1841
10. John Tyler	(Whig)	1841-45
11. James K. Polk	(Democrat)	1845-49
12. Zachary Taylor (Old Rough and Ready)	(Whig)	1849-50
13. Millard Fillmore	(Whig)	1850-53
14. Franklin Pierce	(Democrat)	1853-57
15. James Buchanan	(Democrat)	1857-61
16. Abraham Lincoln (The Rail-Splitter)	(Republican)	1861-65
17. Andrew Johnson	(Republican)	1865-69
18. Ulysses S. Grant	(Republican)	1869-77
19. Rutherford B. Hayes	(Republican)	1877-81
20. James A. Garfield	(Republican)	1881
21. Chester A. Arthur	(Republican)	1881-85
22. Grover Cleveland	(Democrat)	1885-89
23. Benjamin Harrison (Little Ben)	(Republican)	1889-93
24. Grover Cleveland	(Democrat)	1893-97
25. William McKinley	(Republican)	1897-1901
26. Theodore Roosevelt (Teddy)	(Republican)	1901-09
27. William H. Taft	(Republican)	1909-13
28. Woodrow Wilson	(Democrat)	1913-21
29. Warren G. Harding	(Republican)	1921-23
30. Calvin Coolidge (Silent Cal)	(Republican)	1923-29

31. Herbert Hoover	(Republican)	1929-33
32. Franklin D. Roosevelt (FDR)	(Democrat)	1933-45
33. Harry S. Truman (Haberdasher Harry)	(Democrat)	1945-53
34. Dwight D. Eisenhower (Ike)	(Republican)	1953-61
35. John F. Kennedy (JFK)	(Democrat)	1961-63
36. Lyndon B. Johnson (LBJ)	(Democrat)	1963-69
37. Richard M. Nixon (Tricky Dicky)	(Republican)	1969-74
38. Gerald R. Ford	(Republican)	1974-77
39. Jimmy Carter (The Peanut Farmer)	(Democrat)	1977-81
40. Ronald Reagan (The Cowboy)	(Republican)	1981-89
41. George Bush	(Republican)	1989-93
42. Bill Clinton	(Democrat)	1993-2001
43. George W. Bush	(Republican)	2001-

Inventors

Johannes Gutenberg	Printing from Metal Moveable Type	1448
Hans Lippershey	(Refracting) Telescope	1608
John Napier	Logarithms	1614
William Oughtred	Slide Rule	1625
Evangelista Torricelli	(Mercury) Barometer	1643
(Sir) Isaac Newton	(Reflecting) Telescope	1668
Thomas Newcomen	Steam Engine	1705
John Kay	Flying Shuttle	1733
James Hargreaves	Spinning Jenny	1764
James Watt	Steam Engine (development)	1765
(Sir) Richard Arkwright	Water Frame	1769
Samuel Crompton	Spinning Mule	1779
Edmund Cartwright	Power Loom	1785
Joseph-Marie Jacquard	Automatic Loom	1801
Richard Trevithick	Steam Locomotive	1804
(Sir) Humphry Davy	Miner's Safety Lamp	1815
Samuel Morse	Electric Telegraph	1832
Charles Babbage	Mechanical Computer	1835

Samuel Colt	Revolver	1835
Kirkpatrick MacMillan	Bicycle	1839
Elias Howe	Sewing Machine	1846
Walter Hunt	Safety Pin	1849
Isaac Singer	Domestic/Industrial Sewing Machine	1851
Elisha Graves Otis	Passenger Lift (Elevator)	1857
Alexander Graham Bell	Telephone	1876
Thomas Alva Edison	Phonograph	1877
Joseph Swan/Edison	Light Bulb	1878
Lewis E. Waterman	Fountain Pen	1884
John Boyd Dunlop	Pneumatic Bicycle Tyre	1888
Whitcomb L. Judson	Zip Fastener	1891
Guglielmo Marconi	Wireless	1895
King Camp Gillette	Modern Safety Razor	1901
(Sir) Ernest Swinton	Tank	1916
John Logie Baird	Television	1926
Clarence Birdseye	Frozen Food Process	1929
Percy Shaw	Cat's-eyes	1934
(Sir) Robert Watson-Watt	Radar	1935
(Sir) Frank Whittle	Jet Engine	1941
(Sir) Barnes Wallis	Bouncing Bomb	1943
Jacques Cousteau	Aqualung	1943
Ladislao Biro	Ballpoint Pen	1944
Edwin Land	Polaroid Camera	1947
(Sir) Christopher Cockerell	Hovercraft	1955

Assassinations

Victim	*Assassin*	
Julius Caesar	Brutus, Cassius etc.	44BC
Henry IV of Navarre	François Ravaillac	1610
Duke of Buckingham	John Felton	1628
Jean-Paul Marat	Charlotte Corday	1793
Spencer Perceval	John Bellingham	1812
Abraham Lincoln	John Wilkes Booth	1865
James Garfield	Charles Guiteau	1881
William McKinley	Leon Czolgosz	1901
Franz Ferdinand	Gavrilo Princip	1914

Grigori Rasputin	Feliks Yusupov	1916
Leon Trotsky	Ramon Mercader	1940
Mohandas K. Gandhi	Nathuran Godse	1948
John F. Kennedy	Lee Harvey Oswald	1963
Lee Harvey Oswald	Jack Ruby	1963
Martin Luther King	James Earl Ray	1968
Robert Kennedy	Sirhan Bishara Sirhan	1968
John Lennon	Mark David Chapman	1980
Anwar Sadat	Khalid Ahmed Shawki	1981
Indira Gandhi	Beant and Satwant Singh	1984
Rajiv Gandhi	Thanu	1991
Yitzhak Rabin	Yigal Amir	1995

Some Historically Famous Horses

Horse		*Rider*
Bucephalus	–	Alexander the Great.
Incitatus	–	Caligula.
Surrey	–	Richard III.
Rosabelle	–	Mary, Queen of Scots.
Sorrel	–	William III.
Black Bess	–	Dick Turpin.
Marengo	–	Napoleon Bonaparte.
Copenhagen	–	Duke of Wellington.
Burmese	–	Queen Elizabeth II.
	Westerns	
Trigger	–	Roy Rogers.
Champion	–	Gene Autry.
Tony	–	Tom Mix.

The 7 Wonders of the Ancient World

1. The Pyramids, at Gizeh, in Egypt.
2. The Hanging Gardens of Babylon (built by Nebuchadnezzar around 587 BC).
3. The Temple of Artemis (Diana) at Ephesus.
4. The Statue of Zeus (Jupiter) at Olympia.
5. The Mausoleum at Halicarnassus (*c.* 350 BC).
6. The Colossus of Rhodes (a statue of Helios or Apollo, the sun-god – erected 280 BC, destroyed by earthquake 220 BC).
7. The Pharos Lighthouse at Alexandria (built by Ptolemy I *c.* 330 BC).

NB. Only the Pyramids still exist.

RELIGION

Key Facts about World Religions

Bahá'í Faith

Founded in 1863 by Persian visionary Mirza Husain Ali (1817-92) who called himself Bahá'u'lláh (Glory of God). Earlier prophet Mirza Ali Muhammed (1820-50) called himself the Bab (Gateway). Scripture called the *Kitab Akdas*. It is a universal religion emphasizing the value of all religions and is present in almost every country, but particularly in south-west Asia as many of its followers were formerly adherents of Islam. Since 1979 it has been persecuted in Iran.

Buddhism

Founded about 2,500 years ago (*c.* 533 BC) by Prince Gautama Siddharta (563-483 BC) in north-east India. 'Buddha' means 'the Enlightened One'. Main sacred book the *Pali Canon*. Nirvana is the ultimate state to which a Buddhist aspires.

Christianity

Founded nearly 2,000 years ago on the teachings of Jesus Christ (*c.* 4 BC-AD 29). 'Christ' means 'the Anointed One'. His life provided the basis for the New Testament, originally written in Greek. Christianity has the greatest number of adherents in the world today. Its 3 main subdivisions are Roman Catholic, Protestant and the Eastern Orthodox Church. Fundamental belief in a Holy Trinity of Father, Son and Holy Spirit.

Confucianism

Founded about 2,500 years ago by the Chinese philosopher Kong Zi (Kong the Master) known by his Latin name Confucius (*c.* 550-478 BC). His teachings contained in 5 Chinese classics now called the *Analects* (a collection of facts and sayings).

Hinduism

Hindu beliefs originated in the Indus Valley civilization at least 4,500 years ago, making it the world's oldest religion. Hindus worship a triad of 3 chief gods: (1) Brahma – the Supreme Spirit; (2) Vishnu – the Preserver; (3) Rama. Hindu texts called the *Vedas* (knowledge) – earliest text the *Rig Veda* written before 1000 BC. Important ideas include the Transmigration of Souls (reincarnation) and Karma (fate).

Islam

Founded about 1,400 years ago by the prophet Mohammed (Muhammad) AD 570-632. 'Islam' means 'submission' to the will of Allah (God). Holy scripture called the *Koran* (reading). Islamic calendar dates from the Hejira or 'flight' of Mohammed from Mecca to Medina in AD 622. A 'hadj' is a pilgrimage to Mecca, the holiest city of the Moslems (Muslims). Islam is the world's second largest religion.

Judaism

Founded about 4,000 years ago by the Hebrew leader Abraham, who taught his people to worship one God (Jehovah), making Judaism the first truly monotheistic religion. Holy book, the Old Testament, was originally written in Hebrew and begins with the Pentateuch or five books of Moses expounding the Torah (law). Historically, Jews were dispersed throughout the world (the Diaspora) and suffered frequent persecutions (anti-semitism).

Shinto

Ancient Japanese folk religion deriving its ethical principles from Buddhism and Confucianism but having no holy book. 'Shinto' means 'the Way or Doctrine of the Gods'. From the early 6th century AD the Emperor of Japan (the Mikado) was regarded as the religion's god until the idea of divinity was finally renounced officially by Emperor Hirohito in 1946. He then became the constitutional monarch.

Sikhism

Founded in India around AD 1500 by the Guru Nanak (1469-1539), the first of ten gurus (teachers). 'Sikh' means 'disciple'. Main writings contained in the *Adi Granth* (The Original or First Book) compiled by the fifth Guru, Arjun in 1604. Its basis is the Unity of God and the Brotherhood of Man. The Golden Temple at Amritsar is a holy shrine for Sikhs.

Taoism

Chinese philosophical system traditionally said to have been founded by Lao Zi around 600 BC. 'Tao' means 'path' or 'way'. Scriptures, the *Tao-Te Ching* (The Classic of the Way and its Virtue), were probably compiled in the third century BC. Lao Zi advocated choosing above all the path of contentment and harmony with the environment. Later magical side of Taoism represented by the *I Ching* (Book of Changes), a book of divination.

Zoroastrianism

Founded over 3,000 years ago by the prophet Zoroaster (Zarathustra) in Persia. Sacred scriptures, the *Zendavesta*, include the *Gathas*, his philosophical and moral teachings concerning the endless war between the forces of good and evil. Practised by Parsees in north-west India and Iran, it is today the smallest major religion in the world.

Some Religious Movements

	Movement	*Founder*
1534	Society of Jesus (Jesuits).	Ignatius Loyola.
1650	Society of Friends (Quakers).	George Fox.
1738	Methodists.	John Wesley.
1747	Shakers.	James and Jane Wardley.
1827	Plymouth Brethren.	Rev. John Nelson Darby.
1830	Church of Jesus Christ of Latter-Day Saints (Mormons). In 1847 Brigham Young led them to Salt Lake City, Utah.	Joseph Smith.
1872	Jehovah's Witnesses. Founded in Pittsburgh as the International Bible Students Association. Name adopted in 1931 (journals – *The Watchtower/ Awake!*).	Charles Taze Russell.
1879	Christian Scientists (World Church headquarters in Boston USA; journals – *The Citadel /Christian Science Monitor*).	Mary Baker Eddy.
1954	Unification Church (Moonies).	Rev. Sun Myung Moon.

Organizations and Associations

1844	Young Men's Christian Association (YMCA).	(Sir) George Williams.
1865	New Christian Mission. In 1878 name changed to the Salvation Army (motto 'Blood and Fire'; weekly journal – *War Cry*).	William Booth.
1882	Church Army.	Wilson Carlile.

The Bible

The Bible contains altogether **66** books.
The Old Testament contains **39** books (there are **150** Psalms).
The New Testament contains **27** books.
The Apocrypha contains **14** books.
There were **10** Plagues.
There are **10** Commandments.
There were **12** Tribes of Israel.
There were **12** Disciples.
Jesus received **39** lashes.
In the Book of Revelations the number of the beast is **666.**

The magic number **40**:
In the account of Noah's flood it rained for **40** days and **40** nights.
Moses spent **40** days and **40** nights on Mount Sinai before receiving the 10 Commandments.
Moses prayed for **40** days and **40** nights after coming down from Mount Sinai.
The Israelites spent **40** years in the wilderness.
Jesus spent **40** days in the wilderness tempted by the Devil.
The period of Lent is **40** days.

John was called 'the beloved disciple'.
Luke was called 'the beloved physician'.
Matthew was a tax collector.
Paul (Saul of Tarsus) was a tent maker.

Important Saints' Days

February 14th	– Valentine.	September 29th	– Michael.
March 1st	– David.	October 4th	– Francis of Assisi.
March 17th	– Patrick.	October 18th	– Luke.
April 23rd	– George.	October 25th	– Crispin.
April 25th	– Mark.	November 1st	– All Saints.
June 11th	– Barnabas.	November 11th	– Martin.
June 24th	– John the Baptist.	November 30th	– Andrew.
June 29th	– Peter and Paul.	December 6th	– Nicholas.
July 15th	– Swithin.	December 21st	– Thomas.
August 24th	– Bartholomew.	December 26th	– Stephen.
September 1st	– Giles.	December 27th	– John the Evangelist.
September 21st	– Matthew.	December 31st	– Sylvester.

Quarter Days

England		*Scotland (traditional)*	
March 25th	– Lady Day.	February 2nd	– Candlemas.
June 24th	– Midsummer Day.	May (variable)	– Whitsuntide.
September 29th	– Michaelmas.	August 1st	– Lammas.
December 25th	– Christmas Day.	November 11th	– Martinmas.

NB. In 1991 the Scottish quarter days, known as term days, were standardized. While keeping their traditional names, they now occur on February 28th, May 28th, August 28th and November 28th.

Patron Saints

Europe – Benedict.

Patron Saints of Countries

England	– George.	Greece	– Andrew.
Scotland	– Andrew.	Cyprus	– Barnabas.
Wales	– David.	Malta	– Paul.
Ireland	– Patrick.	Sweden	– Eric/Bridget.
France	– Denis.	Denmark	– Canute.
Germany	– Boniface.	Norway	– Olaf.
Austria	– Leopold.	Iceland	– Olaf.
Belgium	– Joseph.	Russia	– Nicholas/Andrew.
Switzerland	– Nicholas.	Czech Republic	– Wenceslas.
Italy	– Francis of Assisi.	Hungary	– Stephen.
Spain	– James (the Great).	Poland	– Stanislas.
Portugal	– Anthony of Padua.	Canada	– Joseph.

Patron Saints of Cities

London	– Paul.	Rome	– Peter.
Edinburgh	– Giles.	Florence	– John the Baptist.
Glasgow	– Kentigern (Mungo).	Venice	– Mark.
Paris	– Geneviève.	Madrid	– Isidore.
Brussels	– Michael.	Lisbon	– Vincent.

THE ROMAN WORLD

Roman Emperors

Augustus Caesar (Gaius Octavius or Octavian) 27 BC-14 AD

The great-nephew and adopted son of Julius Caesar; Augustus became the first Roman Emperor in 27 BC, and the month of August is named after him. He ruled at the time of the birth of Jesus Christ (*c.* 4 BC).

Tiberius 14-37 AD

He ruled at the time of the crucifixion of Jesus Christ (*c.* AD 29).

Caligula (Gaius) 37-41 AD

His nickname means 'Little Boot'. He was an insane tyrant, who is said to have created his favourite horse, Incitatus, a consul. He was murdered by a tribune of the praetorian guard.

Claudius 41-54 AD

A crippled man with a stammer. He invaded Britain in AD 43. He died after eating poisoned mushrooms administered by his physician on the orders of Empress Agrippina.

Nero 54-68 AD

He ruled at the time of the fire which destroyed much of Rome in AD 64. He ordered the executions of St. Peter and St. Paul. Under sentence of death, Nero committed suicide at the age of 30, bringing to an end the Julio-Claudian line of Roman Emperors.

Vespasian 69-79 AD

As a Roman General during the invasion of Britain under Claudius, he conquered the Isle of Wight (Vectis). Following a distinguished military career, he was proclaimed Emperor by his soldiers while campaigning in Palestine. He was a capable administrator, who reorganized the eastern provinces. When dying he is reputed to have said, 'An emperor should die on his feet', and finally, 'Dear me! I think I am turning into a god!' and then dropped dead.

Trajan 98-117 AD

Emperor Nerva adopted him as his heir. He was a fair-minded, conscientious ruler, who conquered Dacia (Romania) and much of Parthia (now north-east Iran). His victories are commemorated by Trajan's Column in Rome.

Hadrian 117-138 AD

Nephew and adopted heir of Trajan. Hadrian is best remembered for the great wall he had built from Wallsend on the Tyne to the Solway Firth (AD 122-126). He was a caring and popular emperor.

Antoninus Pius 138-161 AD

Adopted as Hadrian's heir, he enjoyed a prosperous reign, and is best remembered for initiating the huge earthen wall built between AD 142 and 200 from the Forth to the Clyde as a defence against the Picts.

Marcus Aurelius (Antoninus) 161-180 AD

Nephew and adopted heir of Antoninus Pius. He spent much of his reign fighting various Germanic tribes, despite his peace-loving nature. He was also a Stoic philosopher best remembered for his famous book of *Meditations,* written in Greek.

(Lucius) Septimius Severus 193-211 AD

Proclaimed Emperor by his troops, he proved an able administrator. Following his victory over the Parthians, a triumphal arch was erected in the Roman Forum in his honour. He was the only African to become Emperor and died in York after defeating the Picts.

Diocletian 284-305 AD

Proclaimed Emperor by his troops, he reorganized and sub-divided the unwieldy Roman Empire creating a board of two joint and two subordinate emperors. In 303 he began severe persecution of the Christians, and in 305 he abdicated suddenly in favour of Galerius.

Constantine the Great 306-337 AD

Proclaimed joint-Emperor by the troops following the death of his father Constantius in York in 306, he converted to Christianity after gaining a crushing victory at the Milvian Bridge near Rome in 312. Between 324 and 330 he built a new city at Byzantium on the Bosp(h)orus, and renamed the new capital Constantinople.

Roman Names of English Towns and Cities

Bath	–	Aquae Sulis.
Canterbury	–	Durovernum Cantiacorum.
Carlisle	–	Luguvalium.
Chelmsford	–	Caesaromagus.
Chester	–	Deva.
Chichester	–	Noviomagus.
Cirencester	–	Corinium Dobunnorum.
Colchester	–	Camulodunum.
Doncaster	–	Danum.
Dorchester	–	Durnovaria.
Dover	–	(Portus) Dubris.
Exeter	–	Isca Dumnoniorum.
Gloucester	–	Glevum.
Great Yarmouth	–	Gernemuta Magna.*
Lancaster	–	Lunecastrum.*
Leicester	–	Ratae Coritanorum.
Lincoln	–	Lindum.
Liverpool	–	Esmeduna.*
London	–	Londinium.
Manchester	–	Mamucium (Mancunium).
Newcastle upon Tyne	–	Pons Aelius.
Rochester	–	Durobrivae.
St. Albans	–	Verulamium.
Salisbury (Old Sarum)	–	Sorviodunum.
Southampton	–	Clausentum.
Winchester	–	Venta Belgarum.
Worcester	–	Vigornia.*
York	–	Eboracum.

* NB. Names were applied in post-Roman times.

Roman Names of Islands

Anglesey	–	Mona.	Alderney	–	Riduna.
Isle of Man	–	Manavia.	Guernsey	–	Sarnia.
Isle of Wight	–	Vectis.	Jersey	–	Caesarea.

Roman Names of Countries

England (inc. Wales and S. Scotland)	–	Britannia.
Scotland	–	Caledonia.
Wales	–	Cambria.
Ireland	–	Hibernia.
France	–	Gallia.
Germany	–	Germania.
Greece	–	Graecia.
Italy	–	Italia.
Portugal	–	Lusitania.
Spain	–	Hispania.
Switzerland	–	Helvetia.
Romania	–	Dacia.
Morocco	–	Mauretania.

Roman Numerals

1	–	I	40	–	XL	1,000	–	M
4	–	IV	45	–	XLV	1,500	–	MD
5	–	V	50	–	L	1,900	–	MCM
6	–	VI	90	–	XC	2,000	–	MM
9	–	IX	100	–	C	5,000	–	$\overline{V}$
10	–	X	400	–	CD	10,000	–	$\overline{X}$
19	–	XIX	500	–	D	50,000	–	$\overline{L}$
20	–	XX	600	–	DC	100,000	–	$\overline{C}$
25	–	XXV	900	–	CM	500,000	–	$\overline{D}$
38	–	XXXVIII	990	–	XM	1,000,000	–	$\overline{M}$

MYTHOLOGY

Egyptian Mythology

Character		*Details*
Anubis	–	Jackal-headed god of the dead, son of Osiris.
Apis	–	Bull-headed god of Memphis, linked with Osiris as Serapis.
Horus	–	Falcon-headed god, son of Osiris and Isis.
Isis	–	Wife/sister of Osiris, goddess of fertility.
Nut	–	Goddess of the sky.
Osiris	–	Chief of the gods, embodiment of goodness. He went to rule the Underworld after being killed by Set(h).
Ptah	–	God of creation; chief god of Memphis.
Ra	–	The sun-god.
Set(h)	–	God of night, the desert and evil; portrayed as a grotesque animal.
Thoth	–	Ibis-headed god of wisdom and learning; the supreme scribe.

Greek (Classical) Mythology

Roman counterparts in brackets.

Character		*Details*
Achilles	–	Son of Peleus and Thetis, a Greek warrior killed by a poisoned arrow in his vulnerable heel. The arrow was fired by Paris and guided by Apollo.
Actaeon	–	He inadvertently witnessed Artemis bathing. She turned him into a stag and he was devoured by his own hounds.
Adonis	–	Beautiful youth loved by Aphrodite (Venus).
Aeneas	–	Trojan warrior, son of Anchises and Aphrodite, who escaped destruction of Troy, and whose descendants were responsible for the foundation of Rome.
Aeolus	–	God of the winds.
Agamemnon	–	King of Mycenae, brother of Menelaus and leader of the Greeks in the Trojan War.
Ajax	–	Son of King Telamon. He went mad and slaughtered sheep.
Andromache	–	Trojan princess, wife of Hector.

Andromeda	–	Daughter of Cassiopeia.
Antigone	–	Daughter of Oedipus and Jocasta.
Aphrodite (Venus)	–	Goddess of love.
Apollo	–	The sun-god.
Ares (Mars)	–	God of war.
Argus	–	(1) The builder of the *Argo*. (2) The faithful hound of Odysseus. (3) Creature with 100 eyes, slain by Hermes. Hera then placed his eyes in the tail of her peacock.
Ariadne	–	She helped Theseus escape from the labyrinth and was deserted on Naxos.
Artemis (Diana)	–	Goddess of hunting.
Asclepius (Aesculapius)	–	God of healing.
Athene (Minerva)	–	Goddess of wisdom.
Atlas	–	A Titan who supported the world on his shoulders.
Atreus	–	Father of Agamemnon and Menelaus. His brother, Thyestes, cursed the house of Atreus after being tricked into eating his own sons.
Bellerophon	–	He captured Pegasus with a golden bridle given to him by Athene.
Calypso	–	Nymph who detained Odysseus for seven years.
Cassandra	–	Daughter of Priam and Hecuba. Apollo decreed that her accurate prophecies would never be believed.
Cassiopeia	–	Mother of Andromeda. Poseidon set her image amongst the stars.
Castor Polydeuces (Pollux)	–	The heavenly twins, sons of Zeus and Leda.
Centaur	–	Creature, half man, half horse.
Cerberus	–	3-headed dog who guarded the Underworld.
Charon	–	He ferried dead souls across the river Styx to Hades.
Circe	–	A witch who turned Odysseus' men into swine.
Clytemnestra	–	Twin sister of Helen (of Troy) and wife of Agamemnon, King of Mycenae.
Cronos (Saturn)	–	Father of Zeus.
(The) Cyclops (including Polyphemus)	–	A race of one-eyed giants.
Daedalus	–	Skilful architect who built the labyrinth for King Minos.

Danae	–	Zeus visited her as a shower of gold.
Demeter (Ceres)	–	Goddess of agriculture.
Dionysus (Bacchus)	–	God of wine; son of Zeus and Semele.
Echo	–	She pined away for love of Narcissus.
Electra	–	Daughter of Agamemnon and Clytemnestra, sister of Orestes and Iphigenia.
Endymion	–	Selene caused him to fall into an everlasting sleep so she could always gaze on his beauty.
Eos (Aurora)	–	Goddess of the dawn.
Erebus	–	God of darkness.
Eros (Cupid)	–	God of love, son of Aphrodite (Venus).
Europa	–	Zeus visited her in the form of a white bull.
Eurydice	–	She died from a snake-bite and went down to the Underworld.
(The 3) Fates	–	Female spirits who determined destiny, viz. *Clotho, Lachesis* and *Atropos.*
(The) Furies	–	Winged maidens with serpents twisted in their hair, sometimes called the *Erin(n)yes* or *Eumenides* (kindly ones).
Ganymede	–	Beautiful youth who replaced Hebe as cupbearer to the gods.
Ge/Gaia	–	The Earth.
(The 3) Graces	–	Daughters of Zeus and Hera. 3 goddesses who personified grace and beauty, viz. *Aglaia, Euphrosyne* and *Thalia.*
Hades/Pluto (Dis)	–	God of the Underworld.
Hebe (Juventas)	–	Goddess of youth, daughter of Zeus.
Hecate	–	Goddess of witchcraft and the moon.
Hector	–	Son of Priam who was killed by Achilles.
Helen (of Troy)	–	Wife of Menelaus. 'The face that launched a thousand ships' (Marlowe).
Helios (Sol)	–	God of the sun, identified with Apollo.
Hephaestus (Vulcan)	–	Smith of the gods.
Hera (Juno)	–	Sister/wife of Zeus (Jupiter).
Heracles (Hercules)	–	A hero forced to undertake 12 labours.
Hermes (Mercury)	–	Winged messenger of the gods.
Hermione	–	Daughter of Helen and Menelaus.
Hero	–	High priestess who drowned herself in the Hellespont.

Hestia (Vesta)	–	Goddess of the hearth, sister of Zeus. Temple guarded by Vestal Virgins.
Hippolyta	–	Queen of the Amazons.
Hygieia (Salus)	–	Goddess of health.
Hymen	–	God of marriage, son of Apollo.
Hyperion	–	A Titan. Father of Helios, Selene and Eos.
Hypnos (Somnus)	–	God of sleep.
Icarus	–	Son of Daedalus whose wax wings melted when he ignored his father's advice and flew too near the Sun.
Io	–	Zeus turned her into a heifer.
Iphigenia	–	Daughter of Agamemnon and Clytemnestra, sister of Orestes and Electra.
Irene (Pax)	–	Goddess of peace.
Iris	–	Goddess of the rainbow.
Jason	–	He searched for the Golden Fleece.
Leander	–	Youth of Abydos who swam the Hellespont to visit Hero.
Leda	–	Zeus visited her in the form of a swan.
Medea	–	Sorceress, wife of Jason.
Medusa the Gorgon	–	Her gaze turned men to stone.
Menelaus	–	Son of Atreus, brother of Agamemnon and husband of Helen (of Troy).
Midas	–	King whose touch turned everything to gold and became a curse.
Minotaur	–	Creature, half man, half bull.
(The 9) Muses	–	Daughters of Zeus and Mnemosyne, who presided over the Arts and Sciences; *Calliope* (epic poetry); *Clio* (history); *Erato* (love poetry); *Euterpe* (lyric poetry); *Melpomene* (tragedy); *Polyhymnia* (hymns); *Terpsichore* (dance); *Thalia* (comedy); *Urania* (astronomy).
Morpheus	–	God of dreams, son of Hypnos.
Narcissus	–	Youth whom Artemis caused to fall in love with his own reflection.
Nemesis	–	Goddess of retribution.
Nike (Victoria)	–	Goddess of victory.

Odysseus (Ulysses)	–	King of Ithaca who, after the fall of
	–	Troy, wandered for 10 years.
Oedipus	–	He killed his father and unwittingly married his mother.
Orestes	–	Son of Agamemnon and Clytemnestra.
Orion	–	Mighty hunter changed into a constellation of stars.
Orpheus	–	He received a lyre from Apollo and he married Eurydice.
Pan (Faunus)	–	God of shepherds and flocks.
Pandora	–	First woman on Earth. From her box all the evils of the world flew out leaving only hope as a consolation.
Paris	–	Son of Priam. He abducted Helen, thus beginning the Trojan War.
Pegasus	–	Winged horse which sprang from Medusa's blood.
Penelope	–	Wife of Odysseus.
Persephone (Proserpina)	–	Daughter of Demeter. She married Hades (Pluto).
Perseus	–	Son of Zeus and Danae. He slew Medusa and rescued Andromeda.
Phaedra	–	Sister of Ariadne. She married Theseus.
Plutus	–	God of wealth.
Poseidon (Neptune)	–	God of the sea.
Priam	–	Last King of Troy.
Prometheus	–	He stole the secret of fire from the gods.
Psyche	–	Beautiful maiden who married Eros (Cupid).
Pygmalion	–	King of Cyprus who fell in love with a maiden's statue he had sculpted.
Rhea (Cybele)	–	Mother of Zeus.
Selene (Luna)	–	Goddess of the moon, identified with Artemis.
Theseus	–	Son of Aegeus, King of Athens. He slew the Minotaur.
(The) Titans	–	A race of giants.
Uranus	–	The Heavens.
Zeus (Jupiter)	–	King of the gods.

The Twelve Labours of Heracles (Hercules)

These were tasks set by his despicable cousin Eurystheus, at the behest of the Delphic oracle, to purify Heracles of murder and free him from Hera's clutches.

1. To slay the Nemean lion and bring back its pelt.
2. To slay the Hydra of Lerna, a monster with a dog's body and nine serpent heads.
3. To capture alive the Ceryneian Hind belonging to Artemis.
4. To capture alive the Erymanthian Boar.
5. To cleanse the Augean stables in one day. Heracles did this by diverting two rivers through them.
6. To drive off the man-eating Stymphalian Birds.
7. To capture the Cretan Bull, a magnificent white bull originally sent by Poseidon to King Minos for sacrifice.
8. To fetch the man-eating mares of Diomedes.
9. To acquire the golden girdle of Hippolyta.
10. To steal the cattle of the three-bodied monster Geryon.
11. To fetch the golden apples of the Hesperides.
12. To bring Cerberus up from Hades.

Norse (Scandinavian) Mythology

Character		*Details*
Balder (Baldur)	–	Son of Odin and Frigg(a), husband of Nanna. Much loved god called 'The Beautiful'. He was killed by a twig of mistletoe fired by Hödur at Loki's instigation.
Fafnir	–	Dragon which guarded treasure.
Frey(r)	–	God of fertility and crops.
Frey(j)a	–	Frey's sister and consort of Odin. Goddess of love and night; sometimes confused with Frigg(a).
Frigg(a)	–	Wife of Odin and mother of Thor and Balder. Goddess of married love after whom Friday is named.
Hel(a)	–	Daughter of Loki. She was goddess of the dead and queen of the Underworld.
Hödur (Hoth)	–	Blind god of night who unwittingly killed his twin brother Balder.

Loki	–	God of mischief who contrived Balder's death.
Odin (Woden)	–	Supreme god of battle, wisdom and the atmosphere, who lived in Asgard (home of the gods) where he received the souls of heroes slain in battle and feasted with them in his great hall (Valhalla). Wednesday is named after him.
Thor	–	God of thunder, eldest son of Odin and Frigg(a), after whom Thursday is named.
Tyr (Tiu; Tyw)	–	A war god after whom Tuesday is named.
Valkyries	–	Nine handmaidens of Odin who selected the most valiant of the warriors to die in battle and conducted them to Valhalla.

Hindu Mythology

Character		*Details*
Brahma	–	Creator of the cosmos.
Ganesh (Ganesa)	–	Elephant-headed god of prophesy, son of S(h)iva and Parvati.
Kali	–	Goddess of destruction and death, wife of S(h)iva.
Mahadeva	–	Title given to S(h)iva meaning 'great god'.
Mahadevi	–	Title given to Sakti meaning 'great goddess', worshipped in forms such as Kali or Durva, and in peaceful form as Parvati.
Parvati	–	Consort of S(h)iva and mother of Ganes(h)a.
Rama	–	Incarnation of Vishnu regarded as an example of virtue and morality.
Sita	–	Goddess of agriculture and wife of Rama.
S(h)iva	–	The Destroyer, consort of Parvati.
Ushas	–	Goddess of the dawn.
Vishnu	–	The Preserver whose nine incarnations (human appearances) include such forms as Rama and Krishna.

Arthurian Legends

Arthur	–	Legendary 6th century King and hero of the Britons, said to have been born in Tintagel, Cornwall, and buried in Glastonbury, Somerset.
Avalon	–	Island, identified with Glastonbury since the Middle Ages, to which Arthur's body was transported after his final battle with Mordred.
Bedivere	–	Arthur's last surviving Knight.
Bors	–	Lancelot's cousin; a Knight admitted to the presence of the Holy Grail.
Camelot	–	Legendary seat of King Arthur. In Thomas Malory's *Morte d'Arthur,* his court is at Winchester, but Caerleon in South Wales and Cadbury Castle in Somerset both lay claim to it.
Elaine	–	(1) Daughter of King Pelles and mother by Lancelot of Galahad. (2) The lilymaid of Astolat or the Lady of Shalott.
Excalibur (Caliburn)	–	King Arthur's magic sword. In one version he pulls it from a stone when a boy, whilst in another, he is given it by Vivien, the Lady of the Lake.
Galahad	–	By enchantment, the son of Lancelot and Elaine the Fair. Because of his immaculate purity he succeeds in the quest for the Holy Grail.
Gawain	–	A Knight of the Round Table and the hero of the late 14th century epic poem *Sir Gawain and the Green Knight.*
Guinevere	–	King Arthur's queen whose adulterous liaison with Lancelot in later accounts prevents him completing the quest for the Holy Grail and leads ultimately to Arthur's death, after which she becomes a nun.

Holy Grail	–	The chalice from which Jesus drank at the Last Supper. Joseph of Arimathea was said to have collected Christ's blood in it at the Crucifixion and to have brought it to Glastonbury. King Arthur's Knights sought it because of its supposed supernatural powers.
Igraine (Igerne)	–	Mother of King Arthur.
Iseult (Isolde)	–	Irish princess who was the intended bride of King Mark of Cornwall.
Kay	–	Knight and foster-brother of Arthur.
La(u)ncelot (of the Lake)	–	The most renowned of Arthur's Knights until his love affair with Queen Guinevere brought about the eventual downfall of Arthur's court. His castle was called Joyous Gard. He became a priest after Arthur's death.
Merlin	–	Magician and advisor to Arthur and his father.
Morgan(a) le Fay	–	One of Arthur's sisters. An enchantress, ruler of Avalon who, in one version, heals Arthur after the final battle. In another version, she reveals to Arthur the intrigue between Lancelot and Guinevere, whilst according to Malory she tries to kill Arthur.
Mordred	–	Arthur's wicked nephew who seizes the kingdom in Arthur's absence and is slain by him in the final battle in Cornwall.
Perceval (Parzival)	–	Heroic Knight, the subject of a Wagner opera, who, with Galahad and Bors, is admitted to the presence of the Holy Grail.
Round Table	–	Made by Merlin, originally for Uther Pendragon, it seated 150 Knights and, because of its shape, all places were equal. One seat, the 'Siege Perilous', was reserved for the Knight who would complete the quest for the Holy Grail. A 14th century version of the Round Table can be seen in the Great Hall of Winchester Castle.

Tristram (Tristan)	–	King Mark's nephew who is sent to Ireland to bring back Iseult as a bride for his uncle but, during the journey from Ireland, the couple accidentally drink a love potion binding them inextricably together with tragic consequences. They are the subject of a Wagner opera.
Uther Pendragon	–	King of the Britons and Arthur's father.

GEOGRAPHY

World Physical

Highest Mountains

World/Asia	(1) Everest	Himalayas.
	(2) K2; Chogori; Dapsang; Mt. Godwin Austen	Himalayas.
Western Europe	Mt. Blanc	Alps.
Eastern Europe	Mt. Elbrus	Caucasus.
North America	Mt. McKinley (Alaska)	Rockies.
South America	Aconcagua (Argentina)	Andes.
Africa	(1) Kilimanjaro (Tanzania)	
	(2) Mt. Kenya	
Canada	Mt. Logan (Yukon)	
Australia	Mt. Kosciusko	Australian Alps.
New Zealand	Mt. Cook	Southern Alps.
Japan	Mt. Fujiyama	
England	Scafell Pike	North Pennines.
Scotland/British Isles	Ben Nevis	
Wales	Snowdon	
Ireland	Carrantuohill	

NB. Table Mountain (Cape Town, South Africa);
Sugar Loaf Mountain (Rio de Janeiro, Brazil).

Longest Rivers

World/Africa	– Nile.
S. America	– Amazon.
N. America	– Mississippi-Missouri.
Asia	– Chang Jiang (Yangtze-Kiang).
Europe	– (1) Volga. (2) Danube.
W. Europe	– Rhine.
Australia	– Murray-Darling.
Russia	– Lena.
Canada	– Mackenzie.
England	– Thames.
Scotland	– Tay.
Wales	– Towy.
Ireland/ British Isles	– Shannon.
United Kingdom	– Severn.

Largest Islands

1. Australia (usually regarded as a continent).
2. Greenland.
3. Papua New Guinea.
4. Borneo.
5. Madagascar.

Largest Oceans

1. The Pacific.
2. The Atlantic.
3. The Indian.
4. The Arctic.

Largest Lakes

1. Caspian Sea.
2. Lake Superior.
3. Lake Victoria.
4. Aral Sea.
5. Lake Huron.
6. Lake Michigan.

Largest Deserts

1. Sahara.
2. Australian.
3. Arabian.
4. Gobi.
5. Kalahari.

Some Towns and Rivers of the British Isles

London, Windsor, Oxford (Thames).
Cambridge (Cam).
Southampton (Test, Itchen).
Salisbury, Bath, Bristol (Avon).
Exeter (Exe).
Gloucester, Worcester, Shrewsbury (Severn).
Hereford (Wye).
Rochester, Maidstone (Medway).
Canterbury (Stour).
Chichester (Lavant).
Colchester (Colne).
Ipswich (Orwell).
Northampton, Peterborough (Nene).
Norwich (Wensum).
St. Albans (Ver).
Hertford (Lea).
Bedford, King's Lynn (Great Ouse).
Leicester (Soar).
Derby (Derwent).
Stoke, Nottingham (Trent).
Lincoln (Witham).
Liverpool (Mersey).
Chester (Dee).
Manchester (Irwell).
Preston (Ribble).
Lancaster (Lune).
Doncaster (Don).
Sheffield (Sheaf, Don).
Leeds (Aire).
York (Ouse).
Hull (Humber).
Ripon (Ure).
Middlesbrough, Stockton (Tees).
Durham, Sunderland (Wear).
Newcastle, Gateshead (Tyne).
Carlisle (Eden).
Berwick (Tweed).
Cardiff (Taff).
Swansea (Tawe).
Edinburgh (Firth of Forth).
Glasgow (Clyde).
Balmoral (Dee).
Dundee, Perth (Tay).
Aberdeen (Dee, Don).
Belfast (Lagan).
Dublin (Liffey).
Athlone, Limerick (Shannon).

Natives of British Cities

Aberdonian	– Aberdeen.	Glaswegian	– Glasgow.
Cantabrigian	– Cambridge.	Haligonian	– Halifax.
Cantuarian	– Canterbury.	Liverpudlian	– Liverpool.
Cestrian	– Chester.	Mancunian	– Manchester.
Cicestrian	– Chichester.	Novocastrian	– Newcastle.
Dundonian	– Dundee.	Oxonian	– Oxford.
Dunelmian	– Durham.	Plymovian	– Plymouth.

Counties

Cornishman	– Cornwall.
Lancastrian	– Lancashire.
Salopian	– Shropshire.
Kentish-man	– West Kent (West of Medway).
Man of Kent	– East Kent (East of Medway).

Islands

Manxman	– Isle of Man.
Orcadian	– Orkney (Islands).
Scillonian	– Scilly Isles.

Slang Terms

Brummie	– Birmingham.
Cockney	– London (within the sound of Bow bells).
Geordie	– Newcastle (Tyneside).
Scouser	– Liverpool.

Poetic Names of Countries

Albion	– England.
Cathay	– China.
Emerald Isle	– Ireland.
Land of My Fathers	– Wales.

English Counties

County	*Administrative Capital*
Bedfordshire	– Bedford.
Buckinghamshire	– Aylesbury.
Cambridgeshire	– Cambridge.

County		*Administrative Capital*
Cheshire	–	Chester.
Cornwall	–	Truro.
Cumbria	–	Carlisle.
Derbyshire	–	Matlock.
Devon	–	Exeter.
Dorset	–	Dorchester.
Durham	–	Durham.
East Sussex	–	Lewes.
Essex	–	Chelmsford.
Gloucestershire	–	Gloucester.
Hampshire	–	Winchester.
Hertfordshire	–	Hertford.
Kent	–	Maidstone.
Lancashire	–	Preston.
Leicestershire	–	Leicester.
Lincolnshire	–	Lincoln.
Norfolk	–	Norwich.
Northamptonshire	–	Northampton.
Northumberland	–	Morpeth.
North Yorkshire	–	Northallerton.
Nottinghamshire	–	Nottingham.
Oxfordshire	–	Oxford.
Shropshire	–	Shrewsbury.
Somerset	–	Taunton.
Staffordshire	–	Stafford.
Suffolk	–	Ipswich.
Surrey	–	Kingston upon Thames.
Warwickshire	–	Warwick.
West Sussex	–	Chichester.
Wiltshire	–	Trowbridge.
Worcestershire	–	Worcester.

Counties of Northern Ireland

County		*County Town*
Antrim	–	Belfast.
Armagh	–	Armagh.
Down	–	Downpatrick.
Fermanagh	–	Enniskillen.
Londonderry	–	Londonderry.
Tyrone	–	Omagh.

NB. Since 1996 Scotland has been divided into 32 and Wales into 22 unitary authorities, each with an administrative headquarters.

Europe

Country	*Capital*	*Currency*
England	London	Pound Sterling (£).
Scotland	Edinburgh	Pound Sterling (£).
Wales	Cardiff	Pound Sterling (£).
Northern Ireland	Belfast	Pound Sterling (£).
Rep.of Ireland (Eire)	Dublin	Euro (Eur).
France	Paris	Euro (Eur).
Germany	Berlin	Euro (Eur).
Italy	Rome	Euro (Eur).
Spain	Madrid	Euro (Eur).
Portugal	Lisbon	Euro (Eur).
Belgium	Brussels	Euro (Eur).
Netherlands	Amsterdam	Euro (Eur).
Luxembourg	Luxembourg	Euro (Eur).
Switzerland	Berne	Swiss Franc (S. Fr.).
Liechtenstein	Vaduz	Swiss Franc (S. Fr.).
Austria	Vienna	Euro (Eur).
Norway	Oslo	Krone (N. Kr.).
Sweden	Stockholm	Krona (S. Kr.).
Denmark	Copenhagen	Krone (D. Kr.).
Finland	Helsinki	Euro (Eur).
Iceland	Reykjavik	Krona (I. Kr).
Greece	Athens	Euro (Eur).
Serbia	Belgrade	Dinar.
Croatia	Zagreb	Kuna.
Slovenia	Ljubljana	Tolar.
Macedonia	Skopje	Denar.
Russia	Moscow	Rouble.
Georgia	Tbilisi	Lari.
Ukraine	Kiev	Hryvna.
Belarus	Minsk	Rouble.
Latvia	Riga	Lat.
Lithuania	Vilnius	Litas.
Estonia	Tallinn	Kroon.
Poland	Warsaw	Zloty.
Czech Republic	Prague	Koruna.
Slovakia	Bratislava	Koruna.
Hungary	Budapest	Forint.
Romania	Bucharest	Leu.
Bulgaria	Sofia	Lev.
Albania	Tirana	Lek.
Cyprus	Nicosia	Cyprus Pound.
Malta	Valletta	Maltese Lira.

North America

Country	*Capital*	*Currency*
Greenland	Godthaab (Nuuk)	Danish Krone (D. Kr).
Canada	Ottawa	Canadian Dollar (CA $).
USA	Washington DC	US Dollar (US $).
Mexico	Mexico City	Mexican Peso.

Central America

Belize	Belmopan	Belize Dollar.
Costa Rica	San José	Colón.
El Salvador	San Salvador	Colón.
Guatemala	Guatemala City	Quetzal.
Honduras	Tegucigalpa	Lempira.
Nicaragua	Managua	Gold Córdoba.
Panama	Panama City	Balboa.

South America

Argentina	Buenos Aires	Peso.
Bolivia	La Paz	Boliviano.
Brazil	Brasilia	Real.
Chile	Santiago	Chilean Peso.
Colombia	Bogotá	Colombian Peso.
Ecuador	Quito	US Dollar.
French Guiana	Cayenne	Euro.
Guyana	Georgetown	Guyanese Dollar.
Paraguay	Asunción	Guarani.
Peru	Lima	New Sol.
Surinam(e)	Paramaribo	Guilder.
Uruguay	Montevideo	Peso Uruguayo.
Venezuela	Caracas	Bolivar.

Caribbean Islands

Bahamas	Nassau	Bahamian Dollar.
Barbados	Bridgetown	Barbados Dollar.
Bermuda	Hamilton	Bermudian Dollar.
Cuba	Havana	Cuban Peso.

Country	*Capital*	*Currency*
Dominican Republic	Santo Domingo	Dominican Peso.
Haiti	Port-au-Prince	Gourde.
Jamaica	Kingston	Jamaican Dollar.
Puerto Rico	San Juan	US Dollar.
Trinidad and Tobago	Port of Spain	Trinidad and Tobago Dollar.

Asia

Afghanistan	Kabul	Afghani.
Armenia	Yerevan (Erivan)	Dram.
Azerbaijan	Baku	Manat.
Bangladesh	Dhaka	Taka.
Burma (Myanmar)	Rangoon (Yangon)	Kyat.
Cambodia/Kampuchea	Phnom Penh	Riel.
China	Beijing (Peking)	Renminbi–Yuan.
India	New Delhi	Indian Rupee.
Indonesia	Jakarta	Rupiah.
Iran	Teheran	Rial.
Iraq	Baghdad	Iraqi Dinar.
Israel	Jerusalem	Shekel.
Japan	Tokyo	Yen.
Jordan	Amman	Jordanian Dinar.
Kazakhstan	Astana	Tenge.
Laos	Vientiane	New Kip.
Lebanon	Beirut	Lebanese Pound.
Malaysia	Kuala Lumpur	Ringgit.
Mongolia	Ulan Bator	Tugrik.
Nepal	Kat(h)mandu	Nepalese Rupee.
North Korea	Pyongyang	Won.
Oman	Muscat	Rial Omani.
Pakistan	Islamabad	Pakistan Rupee.
Philippines	Manila	Peso.
Saudi Arabia	Riyadh	Riyal.
South Korea	Seoul	Won.
Sri Lanka	Colombo	Rupee.
Syria	Damascus	Pound.

Country	*Capital*	*Currency*
Thailand	Bangkok	Baht.
Tibet	Lhasa	Renminbi.
Turkey	Ankara	Lira.
U. Arab Emirates	Abu Dhabi	Dirham.
Uzbekistan	Tashkent	Sum.
Vietnam	Hanoi	Dong.

Oceania

Australia	Canberra	Australian Dollar (AU $).
Fiji	Suva	Fiji Dollar.
New Zealand	Wellington	New Zealand Dollar (NZ $).
Papua New Guinea	Port Moresby	Kina.
Western Samoa	Apia	Talà.

Africa

Algeria	Algiers	Dinar.
Angola	Luanda	New Kwanza.
Benin	Porto Novo	Franc CFA.
Botswana	Gaborone	Pula.
Burkina Faso (Upper Volta)	Ouagadougou	Franc CFA.
Cameroon	Yaoundé	Franc CFA.
Chad	Ndjamena	Franc CFA.
Congo	Brazzaville	Franc CFA.
Côte d'Ivoire (Ivory Coast)	Yamoussoukro (former cap. Abidjan)	Franc CFA.
Dem. Rep. of Congo	Kinshasa	Congolese Franc.
Egypt	Cairo	Egyptian Pound.
Ethiopia	Addis Ababa	Ethiopian Birr.
Gabon	Libreville	Franc CFA.
Ghana	Accra	Cedi.
Kenya	Nairobi	Kenyan Shilling.
Lesotho	Maseru	Maluti.
Liberia	Monrovia	Liberian Dollar.
Libya	Tripoli	Libyan Dinar.
Malawi	Lilongwe	Kwacha.
Mauritania	Nouakchott	Ouguiya.

Country	*Capital*	*Currency*
Morocco	Rabat	Dirham.
Mozambique	Maputo	Metical.
Namibia	Windhoek	Namibia Dollar.
Niger	Niamey	Franc CFA.
Nigeria	Abuja (former cap. Lagos)	Naira.
Rwanda	Kigali	Franc.
Senegal	Dakar	Franc CFA.
Sierra Leone	Freetown	Leone.
Somalia	Mogadishu	Somali Shilling.
South Africa	Pretoria/Cape Town	Rand.
Sudan	Khartoum	Dinar.
Swaziland	Mbabane	Lilangeni.
Tanzania	Dodoma (former cap. Dar es Salaam)	Tanzanian Shilling.
The Gambia	Banjul	Dalasi.
Tunisia	Tunis	Dinar.
Uganda	Kampala	New Shilling.
Zambia	Lusaka	Kwacha.
Zimbabwe	Harare	Dollar.

Islands

Island	*Capital*	*Currency*
Madagascar	Antananarivo	Malagasy Franc.
Mauritius	Port Louis	Mauritius Rupee.
Seychelles	Victoria	Rupee.

The United States of America

	State	*Capital*	*Nickname*
1.	Alabama	Montgomery	Cotton State; Heart of Dixie; Yellowhammer State.
2.	Alaska	Juneau	America's Icebox; The Last Frontier; Great Land; Land of the Midnight Sun.
3.	Arizona	Phoenix	Grand Canyon State.

	State	*Capital*	*Nickname*
4.	Arkansas	Little Rock	Wonder State; Land of Opportunity.
5.	California	Sacramento	Golden State.
6.	Colorado	Denver	Centennial State.
7.	Connecticut	Hartford	Constitution State; Nutmeg State.
8.	Delaware	Dover	Diamond State; First State.
9.	Florida	Tallahassee	Sunshine State; Peninsula State.
10.	Georgia	Atlanta	Peach State.
11.	Hawaii	Honolulu	Aloha State.
12.	Idaho	Boise	Gem State; Potato State.
13.	Illinois	Springfield	Prairie State; Land of Lincoln.
14.	Indiana	Indianapolis	Hoosier State.
15.	Iowa	Des Moines	Hawkeye State.
16.	Kansas	Topeka	Sunflower State.
17.	Kentucky	Frankfort	Blue Grass State.
18.	Louisiana	Baton Rouge	Bayou State; Pelican State.
19.	Maine	Augusta	Pine-tree State.
20.	Maryland	Annapolis	Free State; Old Line State.
21.	Massachusetts	Boston	Bay State; Old Colony.
22.	Michigan	Lansing	Wolverine State.
23.	Minnesota	St. Paul	North Star State; Gopher State; Land of a Thousand Lakes.
24.	Mississippi	Jackson	Magnolia State.
25.	Missouri	Jefferson City	Show-Me State.
26.	Montana	Helena	Treasure State.
27.	Nebraska	Lincoln	Cornhusker State; Treeplanter State.
28.	Nevada	Carson City	Silver State; Battle Born.
29.	New Hampshire	Concord	Granite State.
30.	New Jersey	Trenton	Garden State.
31.	New Mexico	Santa Fe	Land of Enchantment.
32.	New York	Albany	Empire State.
33.	North Carolina	Raleigh	Tar Heel State.
34.	North Dakota	Bismarck	Flickertail State; Sioux State; Peace Garden State.

	State	Capital	Nickname
35.	Ohio	Columbus	Buckeye State.
36.	Oklahoma	Oklahoma City	Sooner State.
37.	Oregon	Salem	Beaver State.
38.	Pennsylvania	Harrisburg	Keystone State.
39.	Rhode Island	Providence	Ocean State; Little Rhody; Plantation State.
40.	South Carolina	Columbia	Palmetto State.
41.	South Dakota	Pierre	Coyote State.
42.	Tennessee	Nashville	Volunteer State.
43.	Texas	Austin	Lone Star State.
44.	Utah	Salt Lake City	Beehive State; Mormon State.
45.	Vermont	Montpelier	Green Mountain State.
46.	Virginia	Richmond	Old Dominion State.
47.	Washington	Olympia	Evergreen State.
48.	West Virginia	Charleston	Mountain State.
49.	Wisconsin	Madison	Badger State.
50.	Wyoming	Cheyenne	Equality State.

Other Major Cities of USA

State	*City*	*Features*
Alabama	Birmingham	
California	San Francisco	Golden Gate Bridge; Fisherman's Wharf.
	Los Angeles	Hollywood; Beverly Hills; Universal Film Studios; Disneyland (Anaheim).
	San Diego	Zoo (world's largest); Sea World; Harbour.
Connecticut	New Haven	Yale University.
Florida	Miami	
	Orlando	Disneyworld; John F. Kennedy Space Center (Cape Canaveral); Everglades National Park (Florida).
Georgia	Augusta	US Masters Golf (begun by Bobby Jones 1934).
Illinois	Chicago	Sears Tower.
Kentucky	Louisville	Kentucky Derby (at Churchill Downs).

State	*City*	*Features*
Louisiana	New Orleans	Birthplace of Jazz.
Maryland	Baltimore	
Massachusetts	Cambridge	Harvard University; MIT.
	Plymouth	Pilgrim Fathers landed; Cape Cod.
	Salem	Infamous Witch trials (1692-94).
Michigan	Detroit	Car industry; Tamla Motown.
Missouri	St. Louis	1904 Olympics and World's Fair.
Nebraska	Omaha	
Nevada	Las Vegas	Gambling casinos; entertainment centre.
	Reno	Gambling casinos; quick divorces.
New Jersey	Atlantic City	Gambling city.
	Newark	Airport serving New York.
New Mexico	Albuquerque	
New York	New York City	Empire State Building; UN Headquarters; Radio City Music Hall; Broadway (theatreland).
Ohio	Cincinnati	
	Cleveland	
Oregon	Portland	
Pennsylvania	Philadelphia	Independence Hall; Betsy Ross house; Liberty Bell.
	Pittsburgh	Steel industry.
Tennessee	Memphis	Recording studios and record companies; Graceland (Elvis Presley's home).
Texas	Dallas	Oil; Airport – Dallas/Fort Worth.
	Houston	Headquarters of NASA.
Washington	Seattle	Boeing Aircraft.
Wisconsin	Milwaukee	*Happy Days* set there.

Canada

	Province		*Capital*
1.	Alberta	–	Edmonton.
2.	British Columbia	–	Victoria.
3.	Manitoba	–	Winnipeg.

	Province		*Capital*
4.	New Brunswick	–	Fredericton.
5.	Newfoundland	–	St John's.
6.	Nova Scotia	–	Halifax.
7.	Ontario	–	Toronto.
8.	Prince Edward Island	–	Charlottetown.
9.	Quebec	–	Québec (city).
10.	Saskatchewan	–	Regina.

Territories

Northwest Territories	–	Yellowknife.
Yukon Territory	–	Whitehorse.

Australia

	State		*Capital*
1.	New South Wales	–	Sydney.
2.	Victoria	–	Melbourne.
3.	Queensland	–	Brisbane.
4.	South Australia	–	Adelaide.
5.	Western Australia	–	Perth.
6.	Tasmania	–	Hobart.

Territories

Northern Territory	–	Darwin.
Capital Territory	–	Canberra.

SEA VESSELS

Voyages of Exploration and Discovery

Niña, Pinta and *Santa Maria* (flagship)
Ships used by Christopher Columbus in 1492 on his epic voyage to the West Indies, whose discovery opened up the New World.

Matthew
Ship in which John Cabot discovered Nova Scotia and Newfoundland (England's first colony) in 1497.

Trinidad (flagship) and *Vittoria*
Two of the five ships in which Ferdinand Magellan set sail in 1519. Magellan was killed in the Philippines in 1521, but his lieutenant Sebastian del Cano returned to Seville with 18 surviving sailors aboard the one remaining ship, the *Vittoria,* to complete the first circumnavigation of the globe in 1522.

Pelican (flagship)
Ship, renamed at sea the *Golden Hind*, in which Francis Drake became the first Englishman to circumnavigate the globe (1577-1580). On his return, Drake was knighted on board the *Golden Hind* at Greenwich by Queen Elizabeth I.

Endeavour, Resolution, Adventure and *Discovery*
The ships in which Capt. James Cook made his 3 epic voyages between 1768 and 1779: (1) *Endeavour* (1768-71) – he charted the New Zealand coast and surveyed the east coast of Australia, claiming the island for Britain; (2) *Resolution* and *Adventure* (1772-5) – he became the first man to cross the Antarctic circle; (3) *Resolution* and *Discovery* (1776-9) – he discovered several of the Cook Islands, rediscovered the Hawaiian or Sandwich Islands, but was clubbed to death by natives in Hawaii in 1779.

HMS *Beagle*
Ship which carried a young Charles Darwin on its five year voyage of survey (1831-36) of South America and its islands. Following his study of different species on the Galapagos Islands (belonging to Ecuador), Darwin published his book on evolution, *The Origin of Species by Means of Natural Selection,* in 1859.

Fram
Ship used by Norwegian Arctic explorer Fridtjof Nansen in 1893-95. It can now be seen at Oslo.

Discovery and *Terra Nova*
Capt. Robert Falcon Scott commanded 2 Antarctic expeditions in the *Discovery* (1901-4) and in the *Terra Nova* (1910-12). He reached the South Pole (18th January 1912), a month after the Norwegian explorer Roald Amundsen, but perished on the return journey. The *Discovery* can now be seen at Dundee.

Nimrod, Endurance and *Quest*
Ernest Shackleton commanded 3 Antarctic expeditions: (1) In the *Nimrod* (1907-9) he located the South magnetic pole and climbed Mount Erebus (the world's southernmost active volcano); (2) in 1914-16 he commanded the *Endurance*, which sank in the Weddell Sea; (3) in 1921-22 on his final expedition, Shackleton died on board the *Quest.*

Roosevelt
Ship used by Robert Edwin Peary when he became, at his seventh attempt, the first person to reach the North Pole (6th April 1909).

Kon Tiki
Single-sailed balsa wood raft on which Norwegian anthropologist-explorer Thor Heyerdahl drifted 4,300 miles across the Pacific from Peru to Polynesia in 1947. He was trying to prove his theory that Polynesians came from South America and not southeast Asia. It can now be seen at Oslo.

Ra II
Papyrus raft on which Thor Heyerdahl sailed from Africa to America in 1970. Based on Egyptian and American Indian designs, *Ra II* was intended to show that ancient Egyptians could have crossed the Atlantic in similar fashion thousands of years earlier. It can now be seen at Oslo.

Some Famous Ships

Henri, Grâce de Dieu
Ship which carried King Henry VIII to his historic meeting with King Francis I of France on the Field of the Cloth of Gold outside Calais in 1520.

Mary Rose
Henry VIII's greatest warship, and pride of the Royal Navy, sank in the Solent off Southsea in 1545. Thanks to modern technology, it was recovered 437 years later in 1982, and the remains are now on display at Portsmouth.

Mayflower
Ship in which the Pilgrim Fathers (100 + 2 born at sea) sailed from Plymouth to Cape Cod in 1620 to found the first colony in New England. They originally set sail in the *Mayflower* and *Speedwell* from Southampton but eventually bad weather forced them to take refuge in Plymouth Sound where the *Speedwell* was abandoned.

HMS *Bounty*
In 1789 HMS *Bounty* was involved in the most famous mutiny in naval history when, after obtaining breadfruit trees from Tahiti, Capt. William Bligh and 18 of his crew were set adrift in the Pacific. With only a compass to help him, Bligh safely reached Timor, a journey of 4,000 miles in an open boat. The mutineers led by Fletcher Christian settled on the remote Pitcairn Island, whilst others were caught and hanged.

HMS *Victory*
Horatio Nelson's flagship at the battle of Trafalgar (off Cape Trafalgar, a low headland in SW Spain) on 21st October 1805. Nelson was fatally wounded at the height of the battle by a French sniper on the *Redoutable*. The *Victory* can now be seen at Portsmouth.

HMS *Bellerophon*
Ship on which Napoleon Bonaparte surrendered to the British on 15th July 1815, and which subsequently transported him to exile on St. Helena following his final defeat at the battle of Waterloo (12 miles from Brussels) on 18th June 1815.

The Fighting Temeraire
Its poignant last voyage was captured by the artist J.M.W. Turner in 1839.

SS *Great Western, Great Britain* and *Great Eastern*
3 ships built by the British engineer and inventor Isambard Kingdom Brunel (1806-59): (1) SS *Great Western* (1838) was the first wooden steamship to cross the Atlantic regularly; (2) SS *Great Britain* (1843) was the first large iron hulled screw propeller steamship; (3) SS *Great Eastern* (1858) used paddle wheels as well as a propeller and laid the first transatlantic telegraph cable. The SS *Great Britain* can now be seen at Bristol.

Mary Celeste (Marie Celeste)
US brigantine found mysteriously abandoned in the Atlantic in 1872 with no sign of the crew, but the cargo intact and the saloon cabin laid for tea. The riddle remains unsolved.

Cutty Sark
Built in 1869, the *Cutty Sark* was a famous tea clipper sailing between China and Britain until 1877, and a record-breaking wool clipper sailing to Australia and back from 1883 onwards. The name *Cutty Sark* means 'short chemise' and derives from the witch in Robert Burns' poem *Tam O'Shanter.* Since 1957 the *Cutty Sark* has been permanently preserved in dry dock at Greenwich.

HMS *Warrior*
Built on the Thames in 1860, HMS *Warrior* is the earliest surviving 'Ironclad'. After withdrawal from service she performed various static roles. Following extensive restoration work, the *Warrior* was put on display at Portsmouth in 1987.

HMS *Belfast*
Europe's largest surviving Second World War warship. She is a cruiser which played an active part in the Royal Navy from 1939-1963, and is now to be found on public display moored in the river Thames in London.

HMS *Vanguard*
Britain's largest ever and last battleship (1944-1960).

HMS *Amethyst*
British frigate which in July 1949 made a daring 140 mile dash to safety under cover of darkness along the flooded Yangtze River, four months after being shelled and trapped by advancing Communist armies. She returned to a hero's welcome.

HMY *Britannia*
Ship launched in April 1953 and first put into service in January 1954. The Royal Yacht *Britannia* was designed as a unique royal residence, a royal palace at sea. It also served as a hospital ship in case of need. Its final voyage, begun in January 1997, was to Hong Kong, to be present at the handing back of the colony to China on 30th June 1997. It can now be seen at Leith (Edinburgh's port).

Rainbow Warrior
The international protest ship belonging to the environmental action group, Greenpeace, was badly damaged by two explosions while anchored in Auckland Harbour, New Zealand, in July 1985. Sabotage by French intelligence agents was the suspected cause.

Herald of Free Enterprise
In March 1987, the Townsend Thoresen-owned cross channel car ferry capsized a mile from the Belgian port of Zeebrugge on its way to Dover with considerable loss of life. It rolled over and sank almost certainly because the bow doors were left open, enabling water to pour into the car deck.

Ships of World War II

HMS *Royal Oak*
British battleship sunk at anchor by a German torpedo at Scapa Flow in the Orkney Islands in October 1939.

Graf Spee
German pocket battleship scuttled by her crew off Montevideo harbour after being trapped in the River Plate by the British cruisers *Exeter, Ajax* and *Achilles* in December 1939.

Bismarck
German battleship sunk by British air and naval forces in the North Atlantic in May 1941 in revenge for the sinking of the British battlecruiser HMS *Hood* three days earlier.

HMS *Ark Royal*
Aircraft carrier sunk by an Italian submarine's torpedo in November 1941. (NB. The latest *Ark Royal*, commissioned in 1985, is also an aircraft carrier, and the Royal Navy's largest fighting ship.)

USS *Arizona*
One of several American battleships sunk with great loss of life by the Japanese attack at Pearl Harbour on the Hawaiian island of Oahu on 7th December 1941, prompting the USA to declare war on Japan.

Scharnhorst
German battlecruiser which, with the *Gneisenau* and *Prinz Eugen,* made a daring and successful escape to Germany from Brest via the Channel in February 1942. It was sunk at the Battle of North Cape in December 1943.

Tirpitz
German battleship sunk by RAF bombers in April 1944.

USS *Missouri*
Ship on board which the formal Japanese surrender terms were signed in Tokyo Bay on 2nd September 1945.

The Falklands War (1982)

HMS *Hermes* and HMS *Invincible*
The Royal Naval Task Force sent to the Falkland Islands after Argentina's invasion on 2nd April included 2 aircraft carriers, HMS *Hermes* (flagship) and HMS *Invincible.*

General Belgrano
Argentina's only cruiser was sunk by the submarine *Conqueror* outside a British exclusion zone on the night of 2nd May.

HMS *Sheffield*
Destroyer which became the first British casualty of the conflict when hit by a French-made Exocet missile on 4th May with the loss of 20 men. Other casualties included HMS *Ardent* (21st May), HMS *Antelope* (24th May), HMS *Coventry,* sister ship of the *Sheffield,* and the Cunard container ship *Atlantic Conveyor* (25th May). On 7th June there were Argentine raids on *Sir Tristram* and *Sir Galahad* off Bluff Cove, before a ceasefire was finally agreed on 14th June.

Famous Liners

Titanic
On the night of 14-15th April 1912, the SS *Titanic,* pride of the White Star Line, struck an iceberg in the North Atlantic and sank with the loss of 1,523

lives, including her captain Edward John Smith, while making her maiden voyage. She was at the time the world's largest passenger liner, and considered unsinkable. Controversy surrounds the *Californian* which must have seen the distress rockets but failed to respond and attempt a rescue. At dawn the liner *Carpathia* picked up 705 survivors from the lifeboats. The *Titanic*'s sister ship was called the *Olympic*.

Lusitania
On 7th May 1915 the *Lusitania,* a Cunard liner, was torpedoed without warning by a German submarine and sank with the loss of some 1,200 lives, 8 miles off the coast of Ireland. The 128 American casualties helped to bring the USA into World War One. President Woodrow Wilson abandoned his position of neutrality in April 1917. The *Mauretania,* built in 1907, was the *Lusitania*'s sister ship.

Queen Mary
The *Queen Mary,* built in 1936, the flagship of the Cunard line and the most luxurious ship of its time, transported 1,840 passengers across the Atlantic on each voyage. It is now a floating hotel at Long Beach, California.

Queen Elizabeth
The *Queen Elizabeth,* launched in 1940, caught fire and was destroyed in Hong Kong harbour in January 1972. The liner, a former symbol of Britain's maritime glory, made her last passenger voyage in November 1968, and was the largest ever built.

QEII
The *Queen Elizabeth II*, completed for the Cunard line in 1968, was Britain's largest liner. She is the last large passenger liner to be regularly employed on transatlantic service between Southampton and New York.

Achille Lauro
Italian cruise ship hijacked between Alexandria and Port Said by members of the Palestinian Liberation Organization in October 1985. One elderly, crippled, Jewish passenger was killed, the rest were eventually released. Italy later freed the man who masterminded the hijacking, and the ensuing outcry provoked the fall of Bettino Craxi's Italian government. The ship was ultimately destroyed by fire in November 1994.

Queen Mary 2
Launched in January 2004, the *Queen Mary 2* is now the world's largest passenger liner.

Oil Tanker Disasters

Torrey Canyon

In March 1967, the *Torrey Canyon,* one of the world's largest ships, ran aground off Land's End, spilling its cargo of 100,000 tons of crude oil, and caused massive pollution affecting 100 miles of coastline.

Amoco Cadiz

In March 1978, the super-tanker *Amoco Cadiz* ran aground off the Brittany coast spilling 220,000 tons of crude oil, polluting more than 70 miles of coastline.

Exxon Valdez

In March 1989, the super-tanker *Exxon Valdez* ran aground on a reef off Alaska spilling 12 million gallons of crude oil, causing the worst ecological disaster in US history. The oil slick covered 50 square miles of an area rich in marine wildlife.

Submarines

Nautilus

(1) Submarine designed for Napoleon in 1800 by Robert Fulton.
(2) Name of the world's first nuclear-powered submarine launched by the USA in 1954.

HMS *Dreadnought*

Britain's first nuclear submarine launched in 1960.

HMS *Resolution, Repulse, Renown* and *Revenge*

Four atomic-powered nuclear vessels. The largest submarines ever built for the Royal Navy.

Yachts

Morning Cloud

Yacht owned by former Prime Minister Edward Heath.

Gipsy Moth IV

Yacht in which Francis Chichester became the first Englishman to sail single handed round the world from Britain back to Britain (a voyage of 29,677 miles spending 226 days at sea). On his return he was knighted by Queen Elizabeth II at Greenwich on 7th July 1967 (providing a direct comparison with Francis Drake and Queen Elizabeth I in 1580). *Gipsy Moth IV* was on public display, berthed in Cutty Sark Gardens, Greenwich, between 1968 and 2001, before being put to sea again touring towns around the country.

Lively Lady
Yacht in which Alec Rose sailed single-handed round the world. He landed at Portsmouth, his home town, in his tiny ketch on 4th July 1968 after a journey of 28,500 miles lasting 354 days. He was knighted by Queen Elizabeth II the next day.

Suhaili
Yacht in which Robin Knox-Johnston became the first man to sail non-stop and single-handed round the world. His epic ten month voyage, completed in April 1969, won him the Golden Globe, a trophy offered by the *Sunday Times*.

Maiden
British yacht in which an all-female crew skippered by Tracy Edwards (named Yachtsman of the Year in January 1990) won its class in the second and third legs of the Whitbread Round the World Race.

Lady Ghislaine
Yacht owned by Robert Maxwell from which he mysteriously fell to his death in November 1991.

ENZA New Zealand
Giant catamaran in which an 8-man crew, led by Peter Blake and Robin Knox-Johnston, won the Jules Verne trophy for sailing non-stop round the world in a record time of 74 days 22 hours 17 minutes, returning on lst April 1994.

Kingfisher
Yacht in which 24-year old Ellen MacArthur became the youngest person and fastest woman to sail single-handed round the world when competing in the 2000/2001 Vendée Globe yacht race. Her voyage lasted 95 days.

Watches on Board Ship

Afternoon watch	–	Noon to 4pm.	Middle watch	–	Midnight to 4am.
First dog watch	–	4pm to 6pm.	Morning watch	–	4am to 8am.
Second dog watch	–	6pm to 8pm.	Forenoon watch	–	8am to noon.
First night watch	–	8pm to midnight.			

Sea Areas

Weather forecasts for the Shipping Forecast Areas around the British Isles are broadcast regularly. From north of Scotland clockwise they are as follows: South-East Iceland, Faeroes, Fair Isle, Viking, North Utsire, South Utsire, Cromarty, Forties, Forth, Dogger, Tyne, Humber, Fisher, German Bight, Thames, Dover, Wight, Portland, Plymouth, Biscay, FitzRoy (formerly Finisterre), Sole, Lundy, Irish Sea, Fastnet, Shannon, Rockall, Malin, Hebrides, Bailey.

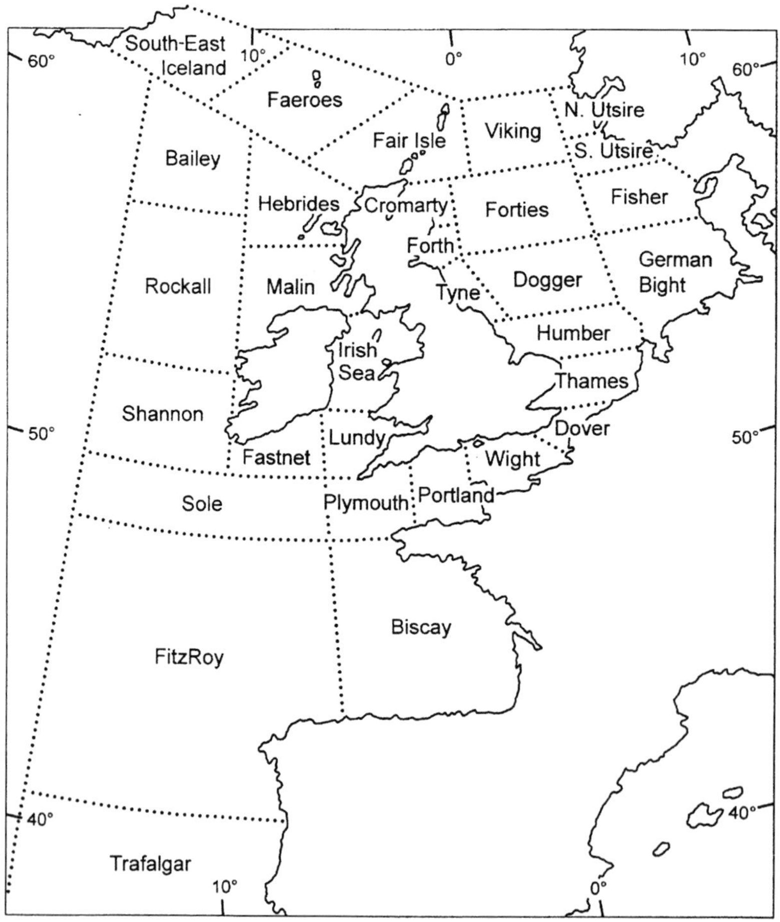

MATHEMATICS

Numbers

A *Fibonacci sequence* is a series of numbers in which each term is the sum of the preceding 2 terms. e.g. 1, 1, 2, 3, 5, 8, 13, 21 etc.

Basic Geometry

Angles

An *acute* angle is less than 90°.
A *right* angle is 90°.
Complementary angles add up to 90°.
An *obtuse* angle is more than 90° but less than 180°.
Supplementary angles add up to 180°.
A *reflex* angle is more than 180°.

Triangles

A triangle is a 3-sided plane figure whose angles total 180°.
An *equilateral* triangle has all 3 sides equal.
An *isosceles* triangle has 2 sides equal.
A *scalene* triangle has no sides equal.

Circles

A circle has 360°.
The *diameter* (d) is a straight line passing through the centre of a circle beginning and ending at the circumference.
The *radius* (r) of a circle is half the diameter.
A *tangent* is a line which touches a circle without intersecting it.
A *segment* is part of a circle cut off by a straight line.
The formula for the circumference of a circle = $2\pi r$ or πd.
The formula for the area of a circle = πr^2.

Plane figures

A *quadrilateral* is any 4-sided figure.
(A *square, rectangle, parallelogram* and *rhombus* all have 4 sides.)
A *pentagon* has 5 angles & sides.
A *hexagon* has 6 angles & sides.
A *heptagon* has 7 angles & sides.
An *octagon* has 8 angles & sides.
A *nonagon* has 9 angles & sides.
A *decagon* has 10 angles & sides.
A *hendecagon* has 11 angles & sides.
A *dodecagon* has 12 angles & sides.

The 5 Platonic solids are

A *tetrahedron*	–	a solid figure with 4 plane faces.
A *hexahedron*	–	a solid figure with 6 plane faces.
An *octahedron*	–	a solid figure with 8 plane faces.
A *dodecahedron*	–	a solid figure with 12 plane faces.
An *icosahedron*	–	a solid figure with 20 plane faces.

COMPUTERS AND COMPUTING

Inside a Computer

Central Processing Unit (CPU)	–	The heart of the computer. A micro-processor which controls all other functions and devices within the computer. Often used as a synonym for the computer itself.
Maths Co-processor	–	Special micro-processor used for speeding up complex mathematical calculations.
Hard Disk/Fixed Disk	–	Electro-magnetic means of providing permanent storage for large amounts of digital information.
Floppy Disk(ette)	–	Electro-magnetic means of providing permanent storage for small amounts of digital information in a form which is easily portable.
Random Access Memory (RAM)	–	Device for storing data on a temporary basis. All information held in RAM is lost when the computer is turned off.
Read Only Memory (ROM)	–	Device for storing small amounts of data permanently. The information can be accessed quickly but cannot be modified by the user of the computer.
Bus	–	Minute tracks used to move information around inside the computer.
Port	–	Socket used to connect a computer to other devices.

Modem	– Device used to enable computers to communicate with one another via telephone lines.
Keyboard/Scanner/Pen/Mouse	– Devices for entering information into a computer.
Visual Display Unit (VDU)	– Screen on which the computer can display its information to the user.

Units of Data

1 Bit	– The smallest unit of data manageable by a computer.
4 Bits	– 1 Nibble.
8 Bits	– 1 Byte (equivalent to a character of information, e.g. 'A').
16 Bits	– 1 word.
1 Kilobyte	– 1 thousand characters of information.
1 Megabyte	– 1 million characters of information.
1 Gigabyte	– 1 billion characters of information.
1 Terabyte	– 1 thousand billion characters of information.

Computer Software

Operating Systems	– Essential software without which no computer will function. It allows other programs to make use of the various components of the computer. The most common operating system for the personal computer is MS-DOS, which stands for Microsoft Disk Operating System.
Spreadsheets	– Software for the easy manipulation of numeric information. Its typical use is for financial modelling. Most common spreadsheets: Microsoft Excel.

Word Processing (WP)	–	Software for the easy manipulation of large volumes of text. It is increasingly used in the world of publishing. Most common WP software: Microsoft Word.
Desktop Publishing (DTP)	–	A more sophisticated form of word processing for complex documents and marketing material.
Database	–	Software for organizing and maintaining large amounts of information for easy retrieval.
Programming Languages	–	Software for developing applications for others to use.

Computer Programming Languages

Algol (***algo****rithmic* ***l****anguage*)
An early high level programming language, developed in the 1950s and 1960s, for scientific applications, but no longer in common use. Despite being a general-purpose language its algebraic style made it most suitable for mathematical work.

Fortran (***For****mula* ***Tran****slation*)
A problem-oriented computer language developed in the mid 1950s. It is one of the earliest languages, and particularly well suited to mathematical and scientific computations.

Cobol (***Co****mmon* ***B****usiness-****O****riented* ***L****anguage*)
A computer programming language developed in the late 1950s especially for commercial use. It aids the writing of programs dealing with business arithmetic and large computer files. It uses English words and is the major language for commercial data processing.

BASIC (***B****eginners* ***A****ll-purpose* ***S****ymbolic* ***I****nstruction* ***C****ode*)
A computer programming language developed in 1971 from Fortran, and based on a combination of simple English and algebra. It uses an interpreter rather than a compiler. Most home computers or micros operate by means of BASIC.

Terminology

Network	– A group of computers connected together in order to be able to share and exchange information with each other.
The Internet	– A global network of powerful computers and networks providing access to services and information for users around the world.
Windows	– Created by the giant software house Microsoft Corporation, the Windows family of operating systems has made it possible for the non-technical user to operate personal computers with ease.
E-Mail	– Electronic Mail is the computer equivalent of the postal service.

Some Abbreviations

AI	–	**A**rtificial **I**ntelligence.
CPU	–	**C**entral **P**rocessing **U**nit.
DTP	–	**D**esk**t**op **P**ublishing.
DVD	–	**D**igital **V**ersatile **D**isk.
EDP	–	**E**lectronic **D**ata **P**rocessing.
HTML	–	**H**yper**T**ext **M**arkup **L**anguage.
HTTP	–	**H**yper**t**ext **T**ransfer **P**rotocol.
ISP	–	**I**nternet **S**ervice **P**rovider.
LCD	–	**L**iquid **C**rystal **D**isplay.
OCR	–	**O**ptical **C**haracter **R**ecognition/ **O**ptical **C**haracter **R**eader.
PC	–	**P**ersonal **C**omputer.
PDF	–	**P**ortable **D**ocument **F**ormat.
SMS	–	**S**hort **M**essaging **S**ervice.
URL	–	**U**niform **R**esource **L**ocator.
VDU	–	**V**isual **D**isplay **U**nit.
WP	–	**W**ord **P**rocessing.
WWW	–	**W**orld **W**ide **W**eb.
IBM	–	**I**nternational **B**usiness **M**achines.
MS-DOS	–	**M**icro**s**oft **D**isk **O**perating **S**ystem.

Well Known Acronyms

GIGO	–	**G**arbage **I**n, **G**arbage **O**ut.
MIPS	–	**M**illions of **I**nstructions **P**er **S**econd.
RAM	–	**R**andom **A**ccess **M**emory.
ROM	–	**R**ead **O**nly **M**emory.
WYSIWYG	–	**W**hat **Y**ou **S**ee **I**s **W**hat **Y**ou **G**et.

PHYSICS

The Spectrum (the 7 colours of the rainbow)

Red, Orange, Yellow, Green, Blue, Indigo, Violet

(mnemonic: **R**ichard **Of** **Y**ork **G**ave **B**attle **In** **V**ain or VIBGYOR).

Thermometers (scales of temperature)

Centigrade or Celsius	–	Water freezes at 0°C/water boils at 100°C.
Fahrenheit	–	Water freezes at 32°F/water boils at 212°F.

To convert from Fahrenheit to Centigrade you subtract 32, divide by 9 and multiply by 5.

To convert from Centigrade to Fahrenheit you divide by 5, multiply by 9 and add 32.

NB. The 2 scales meet at –40°, i.e. –40°C = –40°F.
Normal body temperature is 98.4°F or 36.9°C.
Absolute zero = –273.15°C.

Kelvin	–	Water freezes at 273°K/water boils at 373°K. The Kelvin scale uses absolute zero (–273.15°C) as its starting point (i.e. 0°K) and then continues in degrees Celsius.
Réaumur	–	Water freezes at 0°R/water boils at 80°R.

CHEMISTRY

Chemical Elements and their Symbols

Ag	Silver		
Al	Aluminium	–	most abundant metal in the Earth.
Ar	Argon	–	inert gas.

As	Arsenic	–	a cumulative poison.
Au	Gold		
B	Boron		
Ba	Barium	–	barium sulphate (barium meal) used in digestive tract X-rays.
Br	Bromine	–	halogen; red liquid at room temperature.
C	Carbon	–	hardest element.
Ca	Calcium		
Cl	Chlorine	–	halogen.
Co	Cobalt		
Cr	Chromium	–	makes stainless steel.
Cu	Copper		
F	Fluorine	–	halogen.
Fe	Iron		
H	Hydrogen	–	lightest element.
He	Helium	–	second lightest element; inert gas.
Hg	Mercury	–	liquid, but a metal.
I	Iodine	–	halogen.
K	Potassium	–	metallic element discovered by Sir Humphry Davy.
Kr	Krypton	–	inert gas.
Li	Lithium	–	lightest metal.
Mg	Magnesium		
Mn	Manganese		
N	Nitrogen	–	almost 80% of the atmosphere.
Na	Sodium	–	metallic element discovered by Sir Humphry Davy.
Ne	Neon	–	inert gas.
Ni	Nickel		
O	Oxygen	–	most abundant element on Earth's surface; about 20% of the atmosphere.
Os	Osmium	–	heaviest metal.
P	Phosphorus		
Pb	Lead		
Pt	Platinum		
Pu	Plutonium	–	radioactive element.
Ra	Radium	–	radioactive metallic element discovered by Pierre and Marie Curie (1898).
Rn	Radon	–	inert gas.

S	Sulphur	– brimstone.
Sb	Antimony	
Si	Silicon	– found in sand; used in glass making.
Sn	Tin	
Sr	Strontium	
U	Uranium	– radioactive metal.
W	Tungsten	– wolfram.
Xe	Xenon	– inert gas.
Zn	Zinc	
Zr	Zirconium	

NB. Bessemer process produces steel.
Frasch process produces sulphur.
Haber-Bosch process produces ammonia (NH_3).
Solvey process produces sodium bicarbonate (baking powder).

Ores

Mineral		*Metal*
Bauxite	–	Aluminium.
Cassiterite	–	Tin.
Celestine	–	Strontium.
Cinnabar	–	Mercury.
Galena	–	Lead.
Haematite/Magnetite	–	Iron.
Malachite/Cuprite	–	Copper.
Pentlandite	–	Nickel.
Pitchblende	–	Uranium and Radium.
Sphalerite	–	Zinc.
Wolframite	–	Tungsten.

Alloys

Pinchbeck	–	copper + zinc (small amount).
Brass	–	copper + zinc.
Bronze or Bell Metal	–	copper + tin.
Pewter	–	tin + lead (formerly).

Solder	–	tin + lead (fusible alloy for uniting metals).
Steel	–	iron + carbon.
Stainless Steel	–	iron + carbon + chromium.
Amalgam	–	mercury + another metal.
Paktong	–	nickel-silver.
Permalloy	–	iron + nickel (and other elements).
Sterling silver	–	silver + copper.
Electrum	–	gold + silver (formed naturally).

Chemical Compounds and their Familiar Names

Calcium Carbonate $CaCO_3$	–	Chalk.
Calcium Oxide CaO	–	Quicklime.
Calcium Hydroxide $Ca(OH)_2$	–	Slaked lime.
Hydrous Calcium Sulphate $CaSO_4 2H_2O$	–	Gypsum/ Plaster of Paris.
Nitrous Oxide N_2O	–	Laughing gas.
Nitric Acid HNO_3	–	Aqua fortis.
Sulphuric Acid H_2SO_4	–	Oil of vitriol.
Sodium Chloride $NaCl$	–	Common salt.
Potassium Nitrate KNO_3	–	Saltpetre (nitre).
Hydrated Magnesium Sulphate $MgSO_4 7H_2O$	–	Epsom salts.
Hydrated Sodium Sulphate $Na_2SO_4 10H_2O$	–	Glauber's salt.
Sodium Carbonate Na_2CO_3	–	Washing soda.
Sodium Hydroxide $NaOH$	–	Caustic soda.
Magnesium Hydroxide $Mg(OH)_2$	–	Milk of magnesia.
Magnesium Silicate $Mg_3Si_4O_{10}(OH)_2$	–	Talc.
Natural Hydrated Magnesium Silicate	–	Meerschaum.
Zinc Carbonate $ZnCO_3$	–	Calamine.
Hydrated Ferric Oxide $Fe_2O_3H_2O$	–	Rust.

BIOLOGY

Bones of the Body

Cranium	–	skull.
Malar/Zygomatic bone	–	cheek-bone.
Maxilla	–	upper jawbone.
Mandible	–	lower jawbone.
Clavicle	–	collar-bone.
Scapula	–	shoulder-blade.
Sternum	–	breast-bone.
Humerus	–	upper arm.
Radius	–	lower arm.
Ulna	–	lower arm.
Carpus	–	wrist.
Metacarpus	–	hand.
Pollex	–	thumb.
Phalanges	–	fingers; toes.
Ilium	–	hip.
Femur	–	thigh-bone (longest bone in the body).
Patella	–	knee-cap.
Tibia	–	shin-bone.
Fibula	–	back of leg.
Talus	–	ankle-bone.
Tarsus	–	7 bones of the instep including the Talus.
Metatarsus	–	foot.

NB. An adult human has **206** bones.
There are **12 pairs** of ribs.
There are altogether **33** vertebrae (**7** cervical, **12** thoracic, **5** lumbar, **5** fused vertebrae in sacrum, **4** fused vertebrae in the coccyx).

Anatomical Adjectives

aural	–	of the ear.
brachial	–	of the arm.
buccal	–	of the cheek; of the mouth.
cardiac	–	of the heart.
cerebral	–	of the brain.
cranial	–	of the skull.
digital	–	of the fingers.
genal	–	of the cheeks.
genial	–	of the chin.

haematic	–	of the blood.
hepatic	–	of the liver.
metopic	–	of the forehead.
nasal	–	of the nose.
occipital	–	of the back of the head.
ophthalmic/optic	–	of the eye.
oral	–	of the mouth.
pectoral	–	of the chest.
pedal	–	of the foot.
pulmonary	–	of the lungs.
renal	–	of the kidneys.
tarsal	–	of the ankle.
volar	–	of the palm; of the sole.

Medical Terminology

Erythrocytes	–	red blood corpuscles.
Leucocytes	–	white blood corpuscles.
Phagocytes	–	white blood corpuscles which fight disease by engulfing bacteria.
Herpes Zoster	–	shingles.
Infectious mononucleosis	–	glandular fever.
Parotitis	–	mumps.
Pertussis	–	whooping cough.
Rubella	–	German measles.
Rubeola	–	measles.
Scarlatina	–	scarlet fever.
Varicella	–	chicken pox.
Variola	–	smallpox.
Appendicitis	–	inflammation of the appendix.
Arthritis	–	inflammation of a joint.
Bronchitis	–	inflammation of the lining of the bronchial tubes.
Bursitis	–	inflammation of a bursa, e.g. tennis elbow, housemaid's knee.
Cholecystitis	–	inflammation of the gall bladder.
Colitis	–	inflammation of the colon.
Conjunctivitis	–	inflammation of the conjunctiva.
Cystitis	–	inflammation of the bladder.
Dermatitis	–	inflammation of the skin.

Encephalitis	–	inflammation of the brain.
Fibrositis	–	inflammation of fibrous tissue.
Gingivitis	–	inflammation of the gums.
Glossitis	–	inflammation of the tongue.
Hepatitis	–	inflammation of the liver.
Keratitis	–	inflammation of the cornea.
Laryngitis	–	inflammation of the larynx (voice box).
Mastitis	–	inflammation of the mammary gland.
Meningitis	–	inflammation of the membranes enclosing the brain.
Nephritis	–	inflammation of the kidney.
Neuritis	–	inflammation of the nerves.
Osteitis	–	inflammation of a bone.
Otitis	–	inflammation of the ear.
Peritonitis	–	inflammation of the peritoneum.
Pharyngitis	–	inflammation of the mucous membrane of the pharynx.
Phlebitis	–	inflammation of a vein.
Rhinitis	–	inflammation of the mucous membrane of the nose.
Spondylitis	–	inflammation of a vertebra.
Stomatitis	–	inflammation of the mucous membrane of the mouth.
Tonsillitis	–	inflammation of the tonsils.
Anaemia	–	lack of red blood corpuscles.
Anosmia	–	loss of sense of smell.
Dyspepsia	–	indigestion.
Epistaxis	–	nose bleed.
Hemicrania	–	migraine.
Pollenosis	–	hay fever.
Sternutation	–	sneezing.
Syncope	–	fainting.
Astigmatism	–	eye defect affecting focusing.
Daltonism	–	colour blindness.
Diplopia	–	double vision.
Hypermetropia	–	long-sightedness.
Myopia	–	short-sightedness.

Strabismus	–	squint.
Claudication	–	a limp, lameness.
Traulism	–	stammering, stuttering.

Medical Discoveries

William Harvey	Circulation of the blood	1628
Anton van Leeuwenhoek	Bacteria	1674
William Withering	Digitalis	1785
Edward Jenner	Vaccination against smallpox	1796
Friedrich Sertürner	Morphine	1805
Rudolph Brondes	Atropine	1819
William Morton	Ether as an anaesthetic (first public demonstration)	1846
(Sir) James Young Simpson	Chloroform as an anaesthetic	1847
Louis Pasteur	Pasteurization	1861
(Lord) Joseph Lister	Antiseptic surgery (using carbolic acid)	1865
Robert Koch	Tuberculosis bacillus	1882
Edwin Klebs	Diphtheria bacillus	1884
Louis Pasteur	Rabies (Hydrophobia) vaccine	1885
Wilhelm Röntgen	X-rays	1895
Martinus Bei(r)jerinck	Viruses	1897
Hermann Dreser Felix Hoffman	Aspirin	1899
Jules Bordet	Whooping cough bacillus	1906
Paul Ehrlich	Salvarsan (bacterial agent)	1910
(Sir) Frederick Banting Charles Best	Insulin treatment for diabetes	1922
(Sir) Alexander Fleming	Penicillin	1928
Jonas Salk	Polio vaccine	1952
Luc Montagnier	HIV virus identified	1983

Flowers and Plants

		Common Name
Convallaria	–	Lily-of-the-valley.
Digitalis	–	Foxglove.
Hedera helix	–	Ivy.
Helianthus	–	Sunflower.
Ilex	–	Holly.
Impatiens sultanii	–	Busy Lizzie.
Kniphofia/Tritoma	–	Red-hot poker.
Myosotis	–	Forget-me-not.
Nigella (damascena)	–	Love-in-a-mist.
Saintpaulia	–	African violet.

		Alternative Name
Anemone	–	Wind-flower.
Antirrhinum	–	Snapdragon.
Delphinium	–	Larkspur.
Iris	–	Flag, fleur-de-lis.
Pansy	–	Heart's-ease, love-in-idleness.
Pelargonium	–	Geranium.
(Wild) Clematis	–	Traveller's joy, old man's beard.
(Wild) Geranium	–	Crane's-bill.

PSYCHOLOGY

Important Psychologists

Austrian

Sigmund Freud (1856-1939)
Jewish physician and psychiatrist who originated the technique of psychoanalysis and is regarded as the father of modern psychology. Born in Moravia, he studied and worked in Vienna until 1938 but following the Nazi invasion he was exiled to London where he died. He divided the human personality into three parts which he called the id, ego and superego. His books include *The Interpretation of Dreams, Totem and Taboo* and *The Ego and the Id.*

Alfred Adler (1870-1937)
Psychiatrist, born in Vienna, who broke away from Freud in 1911 and founded the school of individual psychology. He developed the concept of the inferiority complex, believing mankind's main driving force was the desire for power to compensate for feelings of inadequacy. He wrote *Understanding Human Nature.*

Swiss

Carl Gustav Jung (1875-1961)
Psychiatrist from Zürich who broke away from Freud in 1912 and founded his own system which he called analytical psychology. He believed that the collective unconscious was the deepest level of the personality, and developed a 16-category classification of personality types including the introvert and the extrovert. He wrote *Modern Man in Search of a Soul.*

Hermann Rorschach (1884-1922)
Psychiatrist who invented the personality test named after him in which subjects interpret inkblot patterns to help determine their emotional stability, degree of intelligence and personality type.

Jean Piaget (1896-1980)
Educational psychologist whose studies of child development in relation to thought processes have been a strong influence on educational policy.

Russian

Ivan Petrovich Pavlov (1849-1936)

Physiologist, the father of behavioural psychology, who trained dogs by means of conditioning to respond to the sound of a bell. This led to his theory of the 'conditioned reflex' which he regarded as the basis of mental activity.

French

Alfred Binet (1857-1911)

Psychologist who, in collaboration with Theodore Simon, introduced the first reliable intelligence tests in 1905. At Stanford University a modified version, known as the Stanford-Binet Intelligence Scale, was devised and is still used to measure IQ (Intelligence Quotient).

American

John Watson (1878-1958)

Psychologist who founded the school of behaviourism.

Wolfgang Köhler (1887-1967)

German-born American psychologist who was the leader of the *Gestalt* school of psychology which treated behaviour and experience as a whole entity, a view opposed to the behaviourist one.

Burrhus F(rederic) Skinner (1904-1990)

Radical behavioural psychologist who taught at Harvard University and invented the 'Skinner Box', a controlled environment for experiments with animals such as rats, using the technique of conditioned learning reinforced by a reward. He opposed the use of punishment and regarded all behaviour as a conditioned response to outside stimuli. His own daughter was partially reared in a 'baby box' until the age of two.

British

Hans (Jurgen) Eysenck (1916-1997)

German-born English psychologist, a fervent critic of the therapeutic value of psychoanalysis, who adopted a rigorously scientific approach, and developed behaviour therapy in his study of the human personality.

R(onald) D(avid) Laing (1927-1989)

Scottish psychiatrist, a pioneer of radical therapy, who originated the 'social theory' of mental illness. His books include *The Divided Self* and *The Politics of the Family.*

ASTRONOMY

The Planets

Planet	*Satellites*	*Details*
Mercury	None	Nearest to the Sun (36 million miles). Diameter 3,030 miles; 88-day year.
Venus	None	Sometimes called Hesperus (the evening star), Phosphorus (the morning star)/Earth's sister planet. Diameter 7,500 miles; 67 million miles from the Sun; 225-day year. Atmosphere mainly carbon dioxide.
Earth	(1) Moon diameter 2,160 miles	Diameter about 7,925 miles; 93 million miles from the Sun; 365-day year.
Mars	(2) Deimos and Phobos	The Red Planet. Diameter 4,215 miles; 142 million miles from the Sun; 687-day year. NB. In May 2002, water in the form of ice found on Mars.
Jupiter	(61) including Europa, Ganymede, Io and Callisto (these 4 were discovered by Galileo)	The largest planet – it has a Great Red Spot. Diameter 88,700 miles; 483 million miles from the Sun; one revolution takes 12 Earth years. Atmosphere – hydrogen, marsh gas (CH_4) and ammonia (NH_3); temperature reaches -200°C.
Saturn	(31) including Titan (about the size of Mercury) and Phoebe (which revolves in opposite direction to most of the others)	Famous for its rings discovered by Dutchman Christiaan Huygens in 1659. French astronomer Cassini noted divisions in rings in 1675. Diameter 74,500 miles; 886 million miles from the Sun; one revolution takes 29½ Earth years.
Uranus	(21) including Titania, Oberon, Ariel, Umbriel and Miranda	Discovered by William Herschel in 1781. Diameter 32,400 miles; 1,783 million miles from the Sun; one revolution takes 84 Earth years.

Neptune	(11) including Triton and Nereid	Discovered by Johann Gottfried Galle in 1846. Diameter 31,000 miles; 2,793 million miles from the Sun; one revolution takes 165 Earth years.
Pluto	(1) Charon	Discovered by Clyde Tombaugh in 1930. Smallest planet. Diameter 1,400 miles; 3,674 million miles from the Sun; one revolution takes 248 Earth years.

The Asteroid Belt

First discovered at the beginning of the 19th Century, there are now known to be well over 4,000 minor planets or asteroids which orbit the Sun between Mars and Jupiter. They include Ceres (largest), Vesta (brightest), and Eros (discovered in 1898) which comes closer to the Earth than anything other than the Moon, about every 37 years.
NB. Planet means 'wanderer' in Greek.
Comet derives from *coma* which means 'a hair' in Latin.

Speed of Light

Light travels at 186,000 miles per second, (i.e. a beam of light can travel 7½ times around the Earth in one second).

Distances from Earth

The Moon	240,000 miles	(light takes 1.25 seconds).
The Sun	93 million miles	(light takes 8 minutes 14.2 seconds).
Proxima Centauri	25 billion miles (25×10^{12})	(light takes 4.2 years).
Sirius (Dog-Star)	8½ light years	
Vega	26 light years	
Polaris (Pole-Star)	680 light years	

MUSIC

Opera

Composer		*Major Operatic Works*
Italian		
Claudio Monteverdi (1567-1643)	–	Orfeo/The Coronation of Poppea.
Gioacchino Rossini (1792-1868)	–	The Barber of Seville/William Tell/The Silken Ladder/Cinderella/The Thieving Magpie/An Italian Girl in Algiers.
Gaetano Donizetti (1797-1848)	–	Don Pasquale/The Elixir of Love/Lucia di Lammermoor.
Vincenzo Bellini (1801-1835)	–	Norma.
Giuseppe Verdi (1813-1901)	–	Rigoletto/La Traviata/Il Trovatore/Aïda/The Force of Destiny/A Masked Ball/Otello/Falstaff/Macbeth/Don Carlos.
Giacomo Puccini (1858-1924)	–	La Bohème/Tosca/Madame Butterfly/Turandot/Manon Lescaut/Girl of the Golden West/Gianni Schicchi.
Ruggiero Leoncavallo (1858-1919)	–	I Pagliacci.
Pietro Mascagni (1863-1945)	–	Cavalleria Rusticana.
German		
Christoph Gluck (1714-1787)	–	Orpheus and Eurydice.
Ludwig van Beethoven (1770-1827)	–	Fidelio.
Carl Maria von Weber (1786-1826)	–	Der Freischütz/Oberon.
Richard Wagner (1813-1883)	–	Rienzi/The Flying Dutchman/Tannhäuser/Lohengrin (inc. Bridal Chorus)/The Ring of the Nibelung viz. Rhinegold; The Valkyrie; Siegfried; The Twilight of the Gods/Tristan and Isolde/Parsifal/The Mastersingers of Nuremberg.
Engelbert Humperdinck (1854-1921)	–	Hänsel and Gretel.

Richard Strauss (1864-1949)	–	Salome/Elektra/Der Rosenkavalier.
Carl Orff (1895-1982)	–	Carmina Burana.

Austrian

Wolfgang Amadeus Mozart (1756-1791)	–	The Marriage of Figaro/The Magic Flute/ Don Giovanni/Cosi fan tutte/Il Seraglio.
Alban Berg (1885-1935)	–	Wozzeck/Lulu.

French

Jean-Baptiste Lully (1632-1687)	–	Alceste/Armide et Renaud.
Hector Berlioz (1803-1869)	–	The Damnation of Faust/Beatrice and Benedict.
Charles Gounod (1818-1893)	–	Faust/Romeo and Juliet.
Georges Bizet (1838-1875)	–	Carmen/The Pearl Fishers.
Jules Massenet (1842-1912)	–	Manon/Thaïs.
Claude Debussy (1862-1918)	–	Pelléas and Mélisande.

English

Henry Purcell (1659-1695)	–	Dido and Aeneas/The Fairy Queen.
Frederick Delius (1862-1934)	–	A Village Romeo and Juliet.
Benjamin Britten (1913-1976)	–	Peter Grimes/Albert Herring/Billy Budd/ Gloriana/The Turn of the Screw/Noye's Fludde/A Midsummer Night's Dream.

Irish

Michael Balfe (1808-1870)	–	The Bohemian Girl.

Russian

Mikhail Glinka (1804-1857)	–	A Life for the Tsar/Russlan and Ludmilla.
Alexander Borodin (1833-1887)	–	Prince Igor (inc. Polovtsian Dances).

Modest(e) Mussorgsky (1839-1881)	–	Boris Godunov.
Peter Ilyich Tchaikovsky (1840-1893)	–	Eugene Onegin/The Queen of Spades.
Igor Stravinsky (1882-1971)	–	The Rake's Progress.
Serge(i) or (y) Prokofiev (1891-1953)	–	The Love of Three Oranges.

Hungarian

Béla Bartók (1881-1945)	–	Duke Bluebeard's Castle.

Czech

Bedřich Smetana (1824-1884)	–	The Bartered Bride.
Leoš Janáček (1854-1928)	–	The Cunning Little Vixen/Jenufa/From the House of the Dead.

Operettas and Light Operas

German/French

Jacques Offenbach (1819-1890)	–	Orpheus in the Underworld (Can-Can)/ Tales of Hoffmann.

Austrian

Johann Strauss (II) (1825-1899)	–	Die Fledermaus.
Oscar Straus (1870-1954)	–	The Chocolate Soldier.

Hungarian

Franz Lehár (1870-1948)	–	The Merry Widow.

Czech

Rudolf Friml (1879-1972)	–	The Vagabond King.

English

John Gay (1685-1732)	–	The Beggar's Opera/Polly.

W(illiam) S(chwenk) Gilbert (1836-1911) (librettist) (Sir) Arthur Sullivan (1842-1900)	– Thespis/Trial by Jury/The Sorcerer/HMS Pinafore (The Lass that Loved a Sailor)/The Pirates of Penzance (Slave of Duty)/ Patience (Bunthorne's Bride)/Iolanthe (The Peer and the Peri)/Princess Ida (Castle Adamant)/The Mikado (The Town of Titipu)/Ruddigore (The Witch's Curse)/The Yeomen of the Guard (The Merryman and His Maid)/The Gondoliers (The King of Barataria)/Utopia Limited (The Flowers of Progress)/The Grand Duke (The Statutory Duel).
Edward German (Jones) (1862-1936)	– Merrie England.

Classical Composers

Composer	*Well Known Compositions*
English	
(Sir) Edward Elgar (1857-1934) (born Worcester)	– Pomp and Circumstance March (Land of Hope and Glory)/Enigma Variations (inc. Nimrod)/The Dream of Gerontius/The Kingdom/The Apostles/Cockaigne.
Frederick Delius (1862-1934) (born Bradford)	– Mass of Life/Brigg Fair/Requiem.
Gustav Holst (1874-1934) (born Cheltenham)	– The Planets Suite/Egdon Heath/Choral Symphony.
Ralph Vaughan Williams (1872-1958) (born in Gloucestershire)	– 9 Symphonies (inc. 1 Sea; 2 London; 3 Pastoral; 7 Sinfonia Antartica).
(Sir) Arthur Bliss (1891-1975) (born London)	– A Colour Symphony/Checkmate (ballet).
(Sir) William Walton (1902-1983) (born Oldham)	– Crown Imperial/Façade/Belshazzar's Feast/Portsmouth Point/Henry V (film score).
(Sir) Michael Tippett (1905-1998) (born London)	– A Child of Our Time.

Benjamin Britten (1913-1976) (born Lowestoft)	–	Spring Symphony/War Requiem/Let's Make an Opera.

French

Adolphe Adam (1803-1856)	–	Giselle (ballet).
Hector Berlioz (1803-1869)	–	Symphonie Fantastique.
Camille Saint-Saëns (1835-1921)	–	Danse Macabre/Carnival of the Animals.
Léo Delibes (1836-1891)	–	Coppélia; Sylvia (ballets).
Gabriel Fauré (1845-1924)	–	Requiem.
Claude Debussy (1862-1918)	–	L'Après-midi d'un Faune/Clair de Lune/La Mer.
Paul Dukas (1865-1935)	–	The Sorcerer's Apprentice.
Maurice Ravel (1875-1937)	–	Pavane for a Dead Infanta/Daphnis and Chloë; Bolero (ballets).

German

Johann Sebastian Bach (1685-1750)	–	6 Brandenburg Concertos/Christmas Oratorio/St. Matthew Passion/Toccata and Fugue/48 Preludes and Fugues (Well-Tempered Clavier)/Coffee Cantata.
George Frideric Handel (1685-1759)	–	Watermusic/Music for a Royal Fireworks/Largo from Xerxes/Harmonious Blacksmith/Acis and Galatea/Oratorios (inc. The Messiah; Judas Maccabaeus).
Ludwig van Beethoven (1770-1827) (born Bonn; died Vienna)	–	9 Symphonies (inc. 3 Eroica; 5 Fate; 6 Pastoral; 9 Choral)/Egmont Overture/Emperor Concerto/Für Elise.
Felix Mendelssohn-Bartholdy (1809-1847)	–	Wedding March (from A Midsummer Night's Dream)/Hebrides Overture (Fingal's Cave)/Italian, Scottish and Reformation Symphonies/Song Without Words/Hear My Prayer/On Wings of Song.
Robert Schumann (1810-1856)	–	4 Symphonies (inc. 1 Spring; 3 Rhenish)/Humoresque.

Johannes Brahms (1833-1897)	–	4 Symphonies/Academic Festival Overture/ German Requiem/Lullaby/Violin Concerto in D major.
Max Bruch (1838-1920)	–	Violin Concerto in G Minor/Kol Nidrei.
Richard Strauss (1864-1949)	–	Till Eulenspiegel/Also sprach Zarathustra/ Don Quixote/Ein Heldenleben/Don Juan.

Austrian

(Franz) Joseph Haydn (1732-1809) (born Rohrau; died Vienna)	–	104 Symphonies (inc. 45 Farewell; 53 Imperial; 55 Schoolmaster; 83 The Hen; 92 Oxford; 94 Surprise; 96 Miracle; 100 Military; 101 Clock; 103 Drum-Roll; 104 London)/The Creation; The Seasons (oratorios).
Wolfgang Amadeus Mozart (1756-1791) (born Salzburg; died Vienna)	–	41 Symphonies (inc. 31 Paris; 35 Haffner; 36 Linz; 38 Prague; 41 Jupiter)/Eine Kleine Nachtmusik (A Little Night Music).
Franz Peter Schubert (1797-1828) (born and died Vienna)	–	Symphonies (inc. 4 Tragic; 6 Little; 8 Unfinished)/Erl King/Trout Quintet (Die Forelle)/Rosamunde/Lilac Time/A Winter's Journey.
Johann Strauss (1804-1849) Father (born and died Vienna)	–	Radetzky March.
Johann Strauss (1825-1899) Son (born and died Vienna)	–	Blue Danube Waltz/Tales from the Vienna Woods/Thunder and Lightning Polka.
Anton Bruckner (1824-1896) (born Ansfelden; died Vienna)	–	9 Symphonies (inc. 4 Romantic; 8 Apocalyptic).
Gustav Mahler (1860-1911) (born Kalist; died Vienna)	–	10 Symphonies (inc. 1 Titan; 2 Resurrection; 8 Symphony of a Thousand; 10 Unfinished)/Kindertotenlieder.

Italian

Antonio Vivaldi (1676-1741)	–	The Four Seasons.
Luigi Boccherini (1743-1805)	–	Minuet.

Norwegian

Edvard Grieg (1843-1907)	–	Peer Gynt Suite/Holberg Suite/Wedding Day at Troldhaugen.

Finnish

Jean Sibelius (1865-1957)	–	Finlandia/Karelia Suite/The Swan of Tuonela.

Hungarian

Franz Liszt (1811-1886)	–	Hungarian Rhapsodies/Liebestraum.

Czech

Bedřich Smetana (1824-1884)	–	Ma Vlast (My Fatherland).
Antonin Dvořák (1841-1904)	–	9 Symphonies (inc. 5 From the New World)/ Slavonic Dances/Slavonic Rhapsodies/ Stabat Mater.

Polish

Frédéric Chopin (1810-1849)	–	Funeral March/Raindrop Prelude/Fantaisie Impromptu/Revolutionary, Military, Heroic Polonaises/numerous Études, Preludes, Nocturnes and Mazurkas/Les Sylphides/ Minute Waltz.

Russian

Modest(e) Mussorgsky (1839-1881)	–	Pictures at an Exhibition/Night on a Bare Mountain/Song of the Flea.
Peter Ilyich Tchaikovsky (1840-1893)	–	Symphonies (inc. 1 Winter Dreams; 2 Little Russian; 3 Polish; 6 Pathétique)/Manfred Symphony/1812 Overture/Capriccio Italien/ Romeo and Juliet/Nutcracker Suite; Swan Lake; Sleeping Beauty (ballets).
Nikolai Rimsky-Korsakov (1844-1908)	–	Flight of the Bumble Bee/Scheherazade.
Serge(i) or (y) Rachmaninov (1873-1943)	–	3 Symphonies/4 Piano Concertos.
Igor Stravinsky (1882-1971)	–	The Firebird/Petrouchka/The Rite of Spring.

Serge(i) or (y) Prokofiev (1891-1953)	–	Romeo and Juliet (ballet)/Lieutenant Kije suite; Alexander Nevsky (film music)/Peter and the Wolf.
Aram Kha(t)chaturian (1903-1978)	–	Gayaneh (inc. Sabre Dance); Spartacus (ballets).
Dmitri Shostakovich (1906-1975)	–	Leningrad and October Symphonies/First of May.

Musical Theatre

Composer		*Well Known Musicals*
Richard Adler	–	The Pajama Game; Damn Yankees (lyrics – Jerry Ross).
John Barry	–	Billy (lyrics – Don Black).
Lionel Bart	–	Oliver!/Fings Ain't Wot They Used T' Be/ Blitz!/Maggie May.
Irving Berlin	–	Top Hat/Annie Get Your Gun/Call Me Madam. (NB. he also composed the songs 'Alexander's Ragtime Band', 'Always', 'God Bless America', 'White Christmas' and 'Easter Parade').
Leonard Bernstein	–	On the Town/Wonderful Town (lyrics – Betty Comden and Adolph Green)/Candide (additional lyrics – Stephen Sondheim)/ West Side Story (lyrics – Sondheim)/1600 Pennsylvania Avenue (lyrics – Alan J Lerner).
Jerry Bock	–	Fiddler on the Roof; She Loves Me (lyrics – Sheldon Harnick).
Leslie Bricusse	–	Stop the World – I Want to Get Off; The Roar of the Greasepaint – the Smell of the Crowd (lyrics – Anthony Newley)/Pickwick (lyrics only)/Sherlock Holmes – The Musical/ Scrooge.
Cy Coleman	–	Sweet Charity (lyrics – Dorothy Fields)/ Barnum (lyrics – Michael Stewart).
Vivian Ellis	–	Mr Cinders/Bless the Bride (lyrics – A.P. Herbert)/Half in Earnest/Listen to the Wind.
Noël Gay	–	Me and My Girl (lyrics – Douglas Furber)/ Radio Times.
George Gershwin	–	Lady, Be Good (lyrics – Ira Gershwin)/ Porgy and Bess (lyrics – Du Bose Heyward and Ira Gershwin)/Funny Face/Girl Crazy (lyrics – Ira Gershwin)/Oh, Kay!

Ron Grainer	–	Robert and Elizabeth (lyrics – Ronald Millar)/Nickleby and Me (lyrics – Carol Brahms and Ned Sherrin).
Marvin Hamlisch	–	A Chorus Line (lyrics – Edward Kleban)/ They're Playing Our Song (lyrics – Carole Bayer Sager).
(The) Heather Brothers	–	A Slice of Saturday Night/Lust.
David Henneker	–	Half-A-Sixpence/Jorrocks/Phil the Fluter.
Jerry Herman	–	Mame/Hello Dolly/Mack and Mabel/La Cage aux Folles.
John Kander and Fred Ebb (lyrics)	–	Cabaret/Chicago/70 Girls 70/Woman of the Year/The Rink/Kiss of the Spider Woman/ Flora the Red Menace.
Jerome Kern	–	Show Boat (lyrics – Oscar Hammerstein II).
Burton Lane	–	Finian's Rainbow (lyrics – E.Y. Harburg)/ On a Clear Day You Can See Forever (lyrics – Alan J. Lerner).
Frank Lazarus	–	A Day in Hollywood, A Night in the Ukraine (lyrics – Dick Vosburgh).
Mitch Leigh	–	Man of La Mancha (lyrics – Joe Darion).
Alan Jay Lerner (lyrics) and Frederick Loewe	–	Brigadoon/Paint Your Wagon/My Fair Lady/ Gigi/Camelot.
Frank Loesser	–	Guys and Dolls/Hans Christian Andersen/ The Most Happy Fella/How to Succeed in Business Without Really Trying/Where's Charley?
Ivor Novello	–	Glamorous Night/The Dancing Years/ Perchance to Dream/King's Rhapsody.
Stephen Oliver	–	The Life and Adventures of Nicholas Nickleby/Blondel (lyrics – Tim Rice).
Gene de Paul	–	Seven Brides for Seven Brothers (lyrics – Johnny Mercer).
Cole Porter	–	The New Yorkers/The Gay Divorce (filmed as The Gay Divorcée)/Anything Goes/Kiss Me Kate/Can-Can/High Society/Silk Stockings/Nymph Errant.
Richard Rodgers and Lorenz Hart (lyrics)	–	The Boys from Syracuse/Babes in Arms/Pal Joey/On Your Toes.
Richard Rodgers and Oscar Hammerstein II (lyrics)	–	Oklahoma!/Carousel/South Pacific/The King and I/The Flower-Drum Song/The Sound of Music.
Richard Rodgers	–	Do I Hear a Waltz (lyrics – Sondheim).

Sigmund Romberg	– Blossom Time/The Desert Song/The Student Prince.
Willy Russell	– Blood Brothers.
Claude-Michel Schönberg and Alain Boublil (lyrics)	– Les Misérables/Miss Saigon/Martin Guerre.
Harvey Schmidt	– The Fantasticks; I Do! I Do! (lyrics – Tom Jones).
Stephen Schwartz	– Godspell/Children of Eden.
Julian Slade	– Salad Days.
Stephen Sondheim	– A Funny Thing Happened on the Way to the Forum/Anyone Can Whistle/Company/ Follies/A Little Night Music/Pacific Overtures/Sweeney Todd/Merrily We Roll Along/Sunday in the Park with George/Into the Woods/Assassins/Passion.
Charles Strouse	– Applause (lyrics – Lee Adams)/Annie (lyrics – Martin Charnin).
Jule Styne	– Gentlemen Prefer Blondes (lyrics – Leo Robin)/Gypsy (lyrics – Stephen Sondheim)/ Funny Girl (lyrics – Bob Merrill).
Harry Tierney	– Irene (lyrics – Joseph McCarthy).
Harry Warren	– 42nd Street (lyrics – Al Dubin).
(Lord) Andrew Lloyd-Webber and (Sir) Tim Rice (lyrics)	– Joseph and the Amazing Technicolor Dreamcoat/Jesus Christ Superstar/Evita.
(Lord) Andrew Lloyd-Webber	– Tell Me on a Sunday (lyrics – Don Black) and Variations combined as Song and Dance/Cats/Starlight Express (lyrics – Richard Stilgoe)/The Phantom of the Opera (lyrics – Charles Hart)/Aspects of Love (lyrics – Don Black and Charles Hart)/ Sunset Boulevard (lyrics – Don Black and Christopher Hampton)/Whistle Down the Wind (lyrics – Jim Steinman)/The Beautiful Game (lyrics – Ben Elton).
Kurt Weill	– The Threepenny Opera (lyrics – Bertolt Brecht).
Meredith Willson	– The Music Man.
Sandy Wilson	– The Boy Friend/Valmouth/Divorce Me Darling.
Vincent Youmans	– No, No, Nanette! (lyrics – Irving Caesar and Otto Harbach).

Musical Themes

The Beggar's Opera (John Gay)	became	The Threepenny Opera (Kurt Weill).
La Dame aux Camélias/ Camille (Alexandre Dumas)	became	La Traviata (Verdi).
Carmen (Bizet)	became	Carmen Jones (lyrics – Hammerstein II).
Musical Themes including String Quartet (Borodin)	became	Kismet (Robert Wright and George Forrest).
The Importance of Being Earnest (Oscar Wilde)	became	Half in Earnest (Vivian Ellis).
Green Grow the Lilacs (Lynn Riggs)	became	Oklahoma! (Rodgers and Hammerstein).
Liliom (Ferenc Molnár)	became	Carousel (Rodgers and Hammerstein).
The Matchmaker (Thornton Wilder)	became	Hello Dolly (Jerry Herman).

Musicals based on Shakespearian plays

The Comedy of Errors	became	The Boys from Syracuse (Rodgers and Hart).
The Taming of the Shrew	became	Kiss Me Kate (Cole Porter).
Romeo and Juliet	became	West Side Story (Bernstein and Sondheim).
Othello	became	Catch My Soul (Pohlman, Dean and Good).
Macbeth	became	From a Jack to a King (Bob Carlton).
The Tempest	became	Return to the Forbidden Planet (Bob Carlton).

Some operas based on Shakespearian plays

A Midsummer Night's Dream	became	A Midsummer Night's Dream (Benjamin Britten). The Fairy Queen (Purcell).
Much Ado About Nothing	became	Beatrice and Benedict (Berlioz).
The Merry Wives of Windsor	became	The Merry Wives of Windsor (Otto Nicolai). Falstaff (Verdi). Sir John in Love (Vaughan Williams).

Othello	became	Otello (Verdi), Otello (Rossini).
Macbeth	became	Macbeth (Verdi).
Romeo and Juliet	became	Romeo and Juliet (Gounod).

Musicals based on Bernard Shaw's plays

Arms and the Man	became	The Chocolate Soldier (Oscar Straus).
Pygmalion	became	My Fair Lady (Lerner and Loewe).
You Never Can Tell	became	Valentine's Day (Denis King and Benny Green).

Musicals based on Charles Dickens' novels and stories

Oliver Twist	became	Oliver! (Lionel Bart).
Pickwick Papers	became	Pickwick (Cyril Ornadel and Leslie Bricusse).
A Christmas Carol	became	Scrooge (Leslie Bricusse).
A Tale of Two Cities	became	Two Cities (Jeff Wayne).
Nicholas Nickleby	became	Smike (Roger Holman and Simon May). Nickleby and Me (Ron Grainer, Carol Brahms and Ned Sherrin). The Life and Adventures of Nicholas Nickleby (Stephen Oliver).

Films based on Composers' Lives

Ludwig van Beethoven – The Magnificent Rebel.
Irving Berlin – Alexander's Ragtime Band.
Johannes Brahms – Song of Love.
Frédéric Chopin – A Song to Remember.
George Gershwin – Rhapsody in Blue.
Gilbert and Sullivan – The Story of Gilbert and Sullivan/ Topsy-Turvy.
Edvard Grieg – Song of Norway.

George Frideric Handel	–	The Great Mr Handel.
Jerome Kern	–	Till the Clouds Roll By.
Franz Liszt	–	Song Without End/Lisztomania.
Gustav Mahler	–	Mahler.
Wolfgang Amadeus Mozart	–	Amadeus.
Niccolo Paganini	–	The Magic Bow.
Cole Porter	–	Night and Day.
Nikolai Rimsky-Korsakov	–	Song of Scheherazade.
Sigmund Romberg	–	Deep in My Heart.
Franz Schubert	–	Blossom Time (play – Lilac Time).
Robert Schumann	–	Song of Love.
John Philip Sousa	–	Stars and Stripes Forever.
Johann Strauss (II)	–	The Waltz King/The Great Waltz.
Peter Ilyich Tchaikovsky	–	The Music Lovers.

Musical Instructions

Speed: slow → fast

Largo	–	slow and stately.
Lento	–	slowly.
Adagio	–	slow.
Andante	–	at a walking pace.
Moderato	–	moderately.
Allegro	–	quick and lively.
Molto allegro	–	very fast.
Presto	–	very quickly.
Prestissimo	–	(usually) as fast as possible.

Rallentando	–	gradually slowing down.
Accelerando	–	gradually speeding up.

Dynamic: soft → loud

Pianissimo	–	very soft.
Piano	–	soft.
Mezzo piano	–	medium soft.
Mezzo forte	–	medium loud.
Forte	–	loud.
Fortissimo	–	very loud.

Diminuendo	–	gradually getting softer.
Crescendo	–	gradually getting louder.

Character

Con brio	–	with vigour.
Dolce	–	sweetly.
Doloroso	–	sadly.
Giocoso	–	merrily.
Leggiero	–	lightly.
Pesante	–	heavily.
Maestoso	–	majestically.
Scherzando	–	jokingly, playfully.
Vivace	–	lively.

Technical

Attacca	–	go straight on without a break.
Da Capo (DC)	–	return to the beginning.
Arco	–	bowed.
Pizzicato	–	plucked with the fingers.
Glissando	–	slide, sliding.
Legato	–	smoothly.
Staccato	–	detached.
Volta subito (VS)	–	turn the page quickly.
Fine	–	end.

Other terms

Con	–	with.
Senza	–	without.
Molto	–	very.
Poco	–	a little.

Values of Musical Notes

16 semihemidemisemiquavers make a quaver. (rarely used)
8 hemidemisemiquavers make a quaver.
4 demisemiquavers make a quaver.
2 semiquavers make a quaver.
2 quavers make a crotchet.
2 crotchets make a minim.
2 minims make a semibreve (whole-note).
2 semibreves make a breve (double whole-note). (rarely used)

ART

Some Major Art Galleries

London	National Gallery/National Portrait Gallery/Tate Britain/Tate Modern/Wallace Collection/Courtauld Collection, Somerset House.
Liverpool	Walker Art Gallery/Tate Liverpool.
Edinburgh	National Gallery of Scotland.
Glasgow	Burrell Collection.
Paris	Louvre/Musée d'Orsay.
Brussels	Musée des Beaux-Arts.
Amsterdam	Rijksmuseum/Van Gogh Museum.
Madrid	Prado.
Florence	Uffizi/Pitti Palace/Accademia.
Vienna	Kunsthistorisches Museum.
Munich	Alte and Neue Pinakothek.
St. Petersburg (Leningrad)	Hermitage.
New York	Metropolitan Museum of Art/Frick Collection/Guggenheim/ Museum of Modern Art/Whitney Museum.
Washington	National Gallery.
Chicago	Art Institute.

Artists

Artist		*Well Known Paintings*
English		
Nicholas Hilliard (1547-1619)	–	Miniatures (esp. of Elizabeth I).
(Sir) Godfrey Kneller (1646-1723) (German born)	–	Series: Beauties; Portraits of members of the Whig 'Kit Cat Club'.
William Hogarth (1697-1764)	–	Series: Marriage à la Mode; A Rake's Progress; A Harlot's Progress; The Beggar's Opera/Bishop Hoadly/ The Graham Children/Heads of Six Servants/The Roast Beef of Old England/Garrick as Richard III/The Shrimp Girl/Self Portrait with a Pug.

(Sir) Joshua Reynolds (1723-1792)	– Mrs Siddons/Colonel Tarleton/4th Duke of Marlborough.
George Stubbs (1724-1806)	– Paintings of Horses and Dogs.
Thomas Gainsborough (1727-1788) (born Sudbury, Suffolk)	– The Blue Boy/Mrs Siddons/The Morning Walk/Mr and Mrs Andrews/ The Painter's Daughters Chasing a Butterfly/The Watering Place/John Plampin/Dr Ralph Schomberg.
Joseph Wright of Derby (1734-1797)	– An Experiment on a Bird in the Air Pump/The Orrery/Brooke Boothby.
(John) Henry Fuseli (1741-1825) (Swiss born)	– The Nightmare/The Three Witches/ Titania's Awakening/Hamlet and the Ghost/Ariel.
William Blake (1757-1827)	– God Creating Adam/God Judging Adam.
(Sir) Thomas Lawrence (1769-1830)	– Queen Charlotte/George III/George IV/John Julius Angerstein.
J(oseph) M(allord) W(illiam) Turner (1775-1851)	– The Fighting Temeraire/Rain, Steam and Speed/Dido Building Carthage/ Sun Rising Through Vapour/ Burning of the Houses of Parliament/ Interior at Petworth/Chichester Canal/ Crossing the Brook.
John Constable (1776-1837) (born East Bergholt, Suffolk)	– The Haywain/Flatford Mill/Dedham Mill/Salisbury Cathedral/Chain Pier, Brighton/Brighton Beach/The Cornfield/The Cenotaph to Reynold's Memory.
(Sir) Edwin Landseer (1802-1873)	– Dignity and Impudence/The Monarch of the Glen.

Pre-Raphaelite Brotherhood

William Holman Hunt (1827-1910)	– The Scapegoat/The Light of the World/ Our English Coasts (Strayed Sheep)/ Claudio and Isabella/The Hireling Shepherd/The Eve of St. Agnes/The Awakening Conscience/The Triumph of the Innocents/The Finding of the Saviour in the Temple/Valentine Rescuing Sylvia from Proteus.

Dante Gabriel Rossetti (1828-1882)	–	Ecce Ancilla Domini (The Annunciation)/Beata Beatrix/Sir Galahad at the Ruined Chapel/Proserpine/The Girlhood of Mary Virgin.
(Sir) John Everett Millais (1829-1896)	–	Bubbles/Ophelia/Christ in the House of His Parents (The Carpenter's Shop)/The Blind Girl/John Ruskin/ Mariana/Lorenzo and Isabella/ Autumn Leaves/The Return of the Dove to the Ark/The Boyhood of Raleigh.
Ford Madox Brown (1821-1893)	–	The Last of England/Work/'Take Your Son, Sir!'/Pretty Baa-Lambs.
Arthur Hughes (1830-1915)	–	The Long Engagement/April Love.
Henry Wallis (1830-1916)	–	The Death of Chatterton/The Stone-breaker.
(Sir) Edward Burne-Jones (1833-1898)	–	The Beguiling of Merlin/The Mirror of Venus/King Cophetua and the Beggar Maid/Going to the Battle/ The Prioress's Tale/The Mill/Pan and Psyche/The Golden Stairs/ Perseus Slaying the Sea Serpent.
William Morris (1834-1896)	–	Queen Guenevere.
Walter Sickert (1860-1942)	–	Ennui/Bath/The Area Steps/The Evening Primrose/Mamma Mia Poareta.
L(aurence) S(tephen) Lowry (1887-1976)	–	Our Town/Industrial Scene/ Returning from Work/A Fight/Old Property/The Pond.
Paul Nash (1889-1946)	–	The Menin Road/Dead Sea (Totes Meer)/The Battle of Britain.
(Sir) Stanley Spencer (1891-1959)	–	Resurrection Cookham/Swan Upping/ Christ Carrying the Cross.
Graham Sutherland (1903-1980)	–	Somerset Maugham/Sir Winston Churchill.
John Piper (1903-1992)	–	Council Chamber, House of Commons.

Francis Bacon (1909-1992) (Dublin born)	–	Three Studies for Figures at the Base of a Crucifixion.
Lucian Freud (1922-	–	Portrait of Francis Bacon/Various nude studies.
David Hockney (1937-	–	Flight into Italy – Swiss Landscape/ Two Boys in a Pool.

Scottish

Allan Ramsay (1713-1784)	–	Lady Robert Manners/Jean-Jacques Rousseau.
(Sir) Henry Raeburn (1756-1823)	–	Mrs Scott Moncrieff/Rev. Robert Walker Skating on Duddingston Loch.
(Sir) David Wilkie (1785-1841)	–	The Letter of Introduction/Frederick, Duke of York.
William Dyce (1806-1864)	–	Pegwell Bay, Kent, a Recollection of October 5th 1858/George Herbert at Bemerton/Titian's First Essay in Colour/Welsh Landscape with Two Women Knitting.

Welsh

Richard Wilson (1714-1782)	–	View of Snowdon.
Gwen John (1876-1939)	–	Self-portrait/Young Woman in a Red Shawl.
Augustus John (1878-1961)	–	The Smiling Woman/Galway.

American

Benjamin West (1738-1820)	–	Death of General Wolfe.
James Abbott McNeill Whistler (1834-1903)	–	Nocturne in Black and Grey (Whistler's Mother)/Little White Girl (Symphony in White II).
Winslow Homer (1836-1910)	–	Breezing Up/The Boat Builders/ Pitching Quoits/Prisoners from the Front/Waiting for Dad.
John Singer Sargent (1856-1925)	–	Lady Agnew.
Anna Mary 'Grandma' Moses (née Robertson) (1860-1961)	–	Thanksgiving/Moving Day on the Farm.

Edward Hopper (1882-1967)	–	Early Sunday Morning.
Jackson Pollock (1912-1956)	–	Action Paintings.
Roy Lichtenstein (1923-1997)	–	Pop Art.
Andy Warhol (1930-1987)	–	Campbell's Soup/Green Coca-Cola Bottles/Gold Marilyn Monroe.

French

Jean Fouquet (*c*. 1420-1481)	–	Charles VII, King of France.
Jean Clouet (*c*. 1486-1540)	–	King Francis I.
Georges de Latour (1593-1652)	–	St. Mary Magdalen with a Candle/ The Card Players.
Nicolas Poussin (1594-1665)	–	The Adoration of the Golden Calf/ The Adoration of the Shepherds/ Orpheus and Eurydice/The Rape of the Sabines/Bacchanal.
Claude Lorrain(e) (Claude Gellée) (1600-1682)	–	Village Fête/Acis and Galatea/ Cephalus and Procris Reunited by Diana/Flight into Egypt/Seaport with the Embarkation of St. Ursula/ Seaport with the Embarkation of the Queen of Sheba/Landscape with a Rustic Dance/Narcissus/Hagar and the Angel.
Charles Le Brun (1619-1690)	–	Chancellor Seguier.
Antoine Watteau (1684-1721)	–	Gilles/Mezzetin/Embarkation for Cythera.
Nicolas Lancret (1690-1743)	–	Series: The Four Ages of Man; The Four Times of the Day.
Jean-Baptiste Chardin (1699-1779)	–	The Young Schoolmistress/Still Life/The Breakfast Table/Vase with Flowers/The Fountain/Child with Top.
François Boucher (1703-1770)	–	Diana Bathing/Madame de Pompadour.
Jean-Honoré Fragonard (1732-1806)	–	The Swing/Women Bathing.

Jacques Louis David (1748-1825)	–	Madame Récamier/Consecration of Napoleon I/Death of Marat/Death of Socrates/The Oath of the Horatii/The Sabines/Napoleon Bonaparte Crossing the Alps.
Jean-Auguste Ingres (1780-1867)	–	Madame Moitessier/The Turkish Bath/Nude from the Back.
Théodore Géricault (1791-1824)	–	The Raft of the Medusa/The Derby at Epsom 1821/A Horse Frightened by Lightning.
Camille Corot (1796-1875)	–	Avignon from the West.
Paul Delaroche (1797-1856)	–	The Execution of Lady Jane Grey.
Eugène Delacroix (1798-1863)	–	Liberty at the Barricades/The Death of Sardanapalus/Baron Schwiter/The Massacre at Chios/Women of Algiers.
Honoré Daumier (1808-1879)	–	The Washerwoman.
Jean-François Millet (1814-1875)	–	The Gleaners.
Gustave Courbet (1819-1877)	–	Good Morning M. Courbet/The Girls of the Seine Banks/The Burial at Ornans/Stream in a Ravine.

Impressionists

Camille Pissaro (1831-1903)	–	View from Louveciennes/The Louvre in the Snow.
Édouard Manet (1832-1883)	–	A Bar at the Folies Bergère/Lunch on the Grass/The Balcony/Music in the Tuileries Gardens/Olympia/The Barmaid/Portrait of Émile Zola/The Fifer.
Edgar Degas (1834-1917)	–	Absinth Drinkers/Women Ironing/The Ballet Class/At the Races in Front of the Stands/La La at the Fernando Circus.
Alfred Sisley (1839-1899)	–	Flood at Port-Marly.
Claude Monet (1840-1926)	–	Impression: Sun Rising/Waterlilies/Rouen Cathedral/The Beach at Trouville/The Water-Lily Pond.

Pierre Auguste Renoir (1841-1919)	–	The Umbrellas/Moulin de la Galette/ Madame Charpentier and Her Children/The Box/Luncheon of the Boating Party.
Paul Cézanne (1839-1906) *(Post impressionist)*	–	Self Portrait/The Old Lady with the Rosary/Card Players/Still Life/ Bathers/Portrait of His Father.
Henri Rousseau 'Le Douanier' (1844-1910) *(Modern Primitive)*	–	Tropical Storm with a Tiger.
Paul Gauguin (1848-1903) *(Post impressionist)*	–	Tahitian Women/Ia Orana Maria/ The Red Dog.
Georges Seurat (1859-1891) *(Pointillist)*	–	The Circus/La Grande Jatte/Bathers at Asnières.
Henri de Toulouse-Lautrec (1864-1901)	–	At the Moulin Rouge/Jane Avril Dancing/The Female Clown.
Henri Matisse (1869-1954) *(Les Fauves)*	–	The Sisters/The Moroccan/Luxury.
Georges Braque (1882-1963) *(Cubist)*	–	Houses at L'Estaque/Still Life with Violin and Pitcher.
Maurice Utrillo (1883-1955)	–	Scenes of Paris, esp. Montmartre.

Italian

Duccio (di Buoninsegna) (*c.* 1255-1319)	–	Altarpiece for Siena Cathedral/ Virgin and Child with Four Angels.
Giotto (di Bondone) (*c.* 1266-1337)	–	Legend of St. Francis (fresco at Assisi)/Scenes from the lives of St. Joachim & St. Anne; Life and Passion of Christ (frescoes in the Arena Chapel, Padua).
Paolo Uccello (1397-1475)	–	The Rout of San Romano.
Fra Angelico (*c.* 1400-1455)	–	The Coronation of the Virgin.
Fra Filippo Lippi (1406-1469)	–	Frescoes at Prato Cathedral/ Barbadori Altarpiece.
Piero della Francesca (1420-1492)	–	The Baptism of Christ.
Sandro Botticelli ('little barrel') (Alessandro Filipepi) (1445-1510)	–	The Birth of Venus/Primavera (Allegory of Spring)/Madonna and Child/The Mystic Nativity/Venus and Mars/Portrait of a Man/Madonna of the Magnificat/Madonna of the Pomegranate.

Leonardo da Vinci (1452-1519)	–	La Gioconda (Mona Lisa)/The Last Supper/Madonna of the Rocks/The Holy Family with St. Anne/ Adoration of the Magi/The Annunciation/La Belle Ferronière (Portrait of a Lady)/Cartoon: Madonna and Child with St. Anne and John the Baptist.
Filippino Lippi (1457-1504)	–	The Vision of St. Bernard.
Michelangelo Buonarroti (1475-1564)	–	Ceiling of the Sistine Chapel (The Creation)/The Last Judgment (altar wall)/The Holy Family.
Giorgione (*c.*1478-1510)	–	Castelfranco Madonna (altar piece)/ Tempest (Venice).
Raphael (Raffaello Santi) (1483-1520)	–	Madonna of the Goldfinch/Portrait of Julius II/Self Portrait.
Titian (Tiziano Vecelli) (*c.*1483-1576)	–	Noli me tangere/Bacchus and Ariadne/The Urbino Venus/Venus and Adonis/Danae/Philip II of Spain/The Entombment/The Mocking of Christ/The Pilgrims at Emmaus/ The Death of Actaeon.
Antonio Correggio (*c.*1489-1534)	–	Holy Night/Mercury Instructing Cupid/Jupiter and Antiope/The Mystic Marriage of St. Catherine/ Io/Ganymede/Leda.
Jacopo Bassano (Jacopo da Ponte) (*c.*1510-1592)	–	The Miraculous Draught of Fishes/ Jacob's Return to Canaan/Portrait of a Gentleman.
Tintoretto ('little dyer') (Jacopo Robusti) (1518-1594)	–	Bacchus and Ariadne/Origin of the Milky Way/Christ in the House of Mary and Martha/Susanna and the Elders/Flight into Egypt/Christ Washing His Disciples' Feet.
Paolo Veronese (1528-1588)	–	The Wedding Feast at Cana/The Family of Darius Before Alexander/ The Finding of Moses/The Rape of Europa/Allegory.
Caravaggio (*c.*1573-1610)	–	Supper at Emmaus/The Calling of St. Matthew/The Conversion of St. Paul/Bacchus/Salome with the Head of John the Baptist/Boy Bitten by a Lizard.

Giovanni Battista Tiepolo (1696-1770)	–	An Allegory with Venus and Time/ The Banquet of Cleopatra.
Canaletto (Giovanni Antonio Canale) (1697-1768)	–	A Regatta on the Grand Canal/The Basin of St. Marco on Ascension Day/Piazza St. Marco/The Feastday of St. Roch/Upper Reaches of the Grand Canal/The Stonemason's Yard/ Eton College from Across the Thames/Interior of the Rotunda.
Francesco Guardi (1712-1793)	–	The Doge's Palace/Piazza St. Marco.
Giovanni Domenico Tiepolo (1727-1804)	–	The Deposition from the Cross/The Building of the Trojan Horse/The Procession of the Trojan Horse into Troy/The Tumblers.
Amedeo Modigliani (1884-1920)	–	The Cellist.

Greek

El Greco (Domenikos Theotocopoulos) (1541-1614) (born Crete; died Toledo)	–	Christ Driving the Traders from the Temple/The Burial of Count Orgaz/ View of Toledo/Espolio.

Spanish

Diego Velazquez (1599-1660)	–	Las Meninas/Philip IV/The Surrender of Breda/The Rokeby Venus/Old Woman Cooking Eggs/ Pope Innocent X/Topers/Baltasar Carlos.
Bartolomé Esteban Murillo (1617-1682)	–	The Beggar Boy/Boys with Fruit/ The Two Trinities.
Francisco de Goya (1746-1828)	–	Family of Charles IV/3 May 1808/ Maja Nude/Maja Clothed/Colossus/ Duke of Wellington/Dona Isabel de Porcel.
Pablo Picasso (1881-1973) *(Cubist)*	–	Guernica/Les Demoiselles d'Avignon.
Salvador Dali (1904-1989) *(Surrealist)*	–	Christ on the Cross (Crucifixion)/ The Burning Giraffe/The Persistence of Memory.

Flemish

Jan van Eyck (1385-1441)	–	The Arnolfini Marriage/Madonna and Child with Chancellor Rolin/ The Ghent Altarpiece (Adoration of the Lamb).
Rogier van der Weyden (1399-1464)	–	The Descent from the Cross/ Portrait of a Lady.
Hans Memlinc (1430-1494)	–	Man Holding a Medal.
Hieronym(o)us Bosch (1450-1516)	–	The Garden of Earthly Delights and Hell/Ship of Fools/Adoration of the Kings.
Quentin Massys (1464-1530)	–	The Moneylender and His Wife.
Pieter Brueg(h)el the Elder (1525-1569)	–	Hunters in the Snow/Land of Cockaigne/The Tower of Babel/The Peasant Dance/The Fight Between Carnival and Lent/Dulle Griet (Mad Meg).
(Sir) Peter Paul Rubens (1577-1640)	–	Hélène Fourment (his wife)/ Chapeau de Paille/Château de Steen/Arrival of Queen Marie de Medici at Marseilles/Battle of the Amazons/Samson and Delilah/ The Descent from the Cross/The Ceiling of the Banqueting House, Whitehall.
(Sir) Anthony van Dyck (1599-1641)	–	Portrait of Charles I on Horseback/ King Charles I/Triple Portrait of Charles I/Charles I and Henrietta Maria with Their Children/Portrait of Cornelis van der Geest/The Taking of Christ/Madonna of the Rosary/Lamentation for Christ/ Cupid and Psyche/Portrait of Sir Robert Shirley.
David Teniers the Younger (1610-1690)	–	Archduke Leopold-Wilhelm's Gallery/ Temptation of St. Anthony/ Peasants Playing Bowls.

Belgian

Philippe de Champaigne (1602-1674)	–	Triple Portrait of the Head of Cardinal Richelieu/Full length Portrait of Cardinal Richelieu/ The Vision of St. Joseph.
René Magritte (1898-1967) *(Surrealist)*	–	Man with Newspaper/The Two Sisters.

Dutch

Hendrick Avercamp (1585-1634)	–	A Scene on the Ice near a Town/ Frozen River.
Frans Hals (1585-1666)	–	The Laughing Cavalier/The Gipsy Girl/Governesses.
Rembrandt van Rijn (1606-1669) (born Leyden)	–	The Nightwatch/The Anatomy Lesson of Dr Tulp/The Jewish Bride/Family Group/Belshazzar's Feast/The Blinding of Samson/ Christ and the Woman Taken in Adultery/Jacob Blessing the Children of Joseph/Jeremiah Lamenting the Destruction of Jerusalem/Titus (his son)/Various self portraits.
(Sir) Peter Lely (Pieter van der Faes) (1618-1680) (German born)	–	Series of paintings known as Lely's Beauties.
Aelbert Cuyp (1620-1691)	–	View of Dordrecht/River Landscape.
Jan Steen (1626-1679)	–	Skittle Players/The Morning Toilet/ The Village School.
Jacob van Ruisdael (1628-1682)	–	Landscape with a Ruined Castle.
Gabriel Metsu (1629-1667)	–	The Sick Child.
Pieter de Hoogh (1629-1684)	–	The Courtyard of a House in Delft/ An Interior Scene.
Johannes Vermeer (1632-1675)	–	The Artist in his Studio/Girl Reading by an Open Window/View of Delft/A Young Woman Standing and Seated at a Virginal.

Meyndert Hobbema (1638-1709)	–	The Avenue, Middleharnis.
Vincent van Gogh (1853-1890)	–	Sunflowers/Irises/A Cornfield with Cypresses/The Chair and the Pipe/ Church at Auvers/Self Portrait with Bandaged Ear/The Potato Eaters/Starry Night.
Piet Mondrian (1872-1944)	–	Red Tree/Boogie-Woogie.

German

Albrecht Dürer (1471-1528)	–	Self Portrait/Adoration of the Magi.
Hans Holbein the Younger (1497-1543)	–	The Ambassadors/Henry VIII/Jane Seymour/Anne of Cleves/Sir Thomas More/Erasmus/Christina of Denmark.
Caspar David Friedrich (1774-1840)	–	The Cross in the Mountains/Wreck of the 'Hope'.

Austrian

Gustav Klimt (1862-1918)	–	Portrait of Hermine Gallia/The Kiss (mosaic).
Oskar Kokoschka (1886-1980) *(Expressionist)*	–	The Bride of the Wind/Friends/ Saxonian Landscape/Venice/Terrace in Richmond/The Matterhorn.

Swiss

Angelica Kauffman(n) (1741-1807)	–	Self Portrait: Hesitating Between the Arts of Music and Painting/A Lady in Turkish Dress/Penelope at Her Loom/Bacchus Teaching the Nymphs to Make Verses/The Return of Telemachus.
Ferdinand Hodler (1853-1918)	–	The Return from Marignano/William Tell/Night/Day.
Paul Klee (1879-1940)	–	The Creator/Dream Birds/The Fish/ Fool in a Trance/The Ghost Vanishes/Death and Fire.

Norwegian

Edvard Munch (1863-1944)	–	The Scream/The Kiss.

Russian

Wassily Kandinsky (1866-1944) *(Expressionist)*	–	Abstract Paintings, e.g. Composition VII/Der blaue Reiter.
Marc Chagall (1887-1985)	–	Double Portrait/I and the Village/ White Crucifixion/Self Portrait with Seven Fingers/Adam and Eve/ Promenade.

SCULPTURE

Sculptor		*Well Known Sculptures*
Donatello (1386-1466)	–	David.
Michelangelo Buonarroti (1475-1564)	–	David/Pietà/Moses and the Slaves.
Antonio Canova (1757-1822)	–	The Three Graces/Cupid and Psyche/ Pauline Borghese/Napoleon Bonaparte.
Edward Hodges Baily (1788-1867)	–	Statue of Nelson (Trafalgar Square)/Sir Robert Peel/Busts of Samuel Johnson and Sir Isaac Newton.
(Sir) Edwin Henry Landseer (1802-1873)	–	Lions at the base of Nelson's Column.
Edgar Degas (1834-1917)	–	Little Dancer.
Auguste Rodin (1840-1917)	–	Le Penseur (The Thinker)/Le Baiser (The Kiss)/Les Bourgeois de Calais (The Burghers of Calais)/Balzac/Romeo and Juliet.
Alfred Gilbert (1854-1934)	–	Eros (Piccadilly Circus).
Constantin Brancusi (1876-1957)	–	Bird in Space/King of Kings/Colonne Sans Fin.
(Sir) Jacob Epstein (1880-1959)	–	Christ in Majesty (aluminium)/St. Michael and the Devil/Madonna and Child/Genesis/ Ecce Homo/Adam/Lucifer.
Henry Moore (1898-1986)	–	Family Group/Mother and Child/Reclining Figure/Warrior with Shield.
Alberto Giacometti (1901-1966)	–	The Couple/Spoon-Woman/Man Pointing/ Seven Figures and a Head.
(Dame) Barbara Hepworth (1903-1975)	–	Two Figures/Square with Two Circles.
Antony Gormley (1950-	–	The Angel of the North.

ARCHITECTURE

Architectural Styles

1. *Classical* (16th-2nd century BC).
The three orders of *Classical Greek* architecture are *Doric, Ionic* and *Corinthian.* The finest example of *Doric* architecture is the Parthenon, on the Acropolis in Athens, built between 447 and 438 BC under the supervision of Phidias. The architects were Callicrates and Ictinus. Note: the Romans added the *Tuscan* and *Composite* orders to the Greek system, making five in all.

2. *Byzantine* (4th century AD onwards).
Christian architecture with churches based on the Greek cross plan. Examples include St. Mark's, Venice and the Hagia Sophia in Istanbul.

3. *Islamic* (7th century onwards).
Moorish occupation of Spain led to buildings such as the Alhambra (Arabic for 'red') in Granada and the Great Mosque in Cordoba.

4. *Romanesque* (8th-12th centuries).
Western Christian architecture of this period is marked by round arches, circular pillars and barrel vaulting. In England this was characterized by *Norman* 11th and 12th century architecture, e.g. Chichester and Durham Cathedrals.

5. *Gothic* (12th-16th century).
This style originated in Normandy and Burgundy in France, and is characterized by pointed arches, flying buttresses and ribbed vaulting, especially where religious buildings are concerned. It is divided into *Early Gothic* (1130-90), e.g. Notre Dame Cathedral in Paris, *High Gothic* (1190-1350), e.g. Chartres Cathedral, and *Late Gothic* or *Flamboyant* (1350-1520), e.g. Milan Cathedral. The English equivalents are *Early English* (1200-75), e.g. Salisbury Cathedral, *Decorated* (1300-75), e.g. Wells Cathedral and York Minster, and *Perpendicular* (1400-1575), e.g. Winchester Cathedral, Eton College Chapel and King's College Chapel, Cambridge.

6. *Renaissance* (15th and 16th centuries).
A rebirth of Classical architecture represented by the Neo-Classical movement. Important Italian architects included Brunelleschi, Bramante, Michelangelo and Palladio, whose Palladian style was represented in England

by Inigo Jones. Important examples include the Dome of Florence Cathedral (Brunelleschi), St. Peter's, Rome (Michelangelo and Bramante), the Church of San Giorgio Maggiore in Venice (Palladio), and the Queen's House, Greenwich (Inigo Jones).

7. *Baroque* (17th and 18th century).
A very extravagant and flamboyant style of architecture, characterized by architects such as Bernini and Borromini in Rome, and Sir Christopher Wren, Sir John Vanbrugh and Nicholas Hawksmoor in England. The final stage called *Rococo* is characterized by even greater extravagance including the use of motifs such as shells, flowers and trees.

8. *Neo-Classical* (18th and 19th century).
A return to classical principles exemplified in the work of Robert Adam, John Nash and Baron Haussmann. In Britain, Ireland and the colonies it was called *Georgian* (1714-1830) and incorporated the *Regency* style (historically the period 1811-20 but in fact corresponding with the latter part of the 18th century and the early part of the 19th century). Some of the finest examples of *Georgian* architecture are to be found in Bath, such as The Circus (designed by John Wood the Elder and completed by his son) and Royal Crescent and the Assembly Rooms (both designed by John Wood the Younger). Among the best known exponents of *Regency* style architecture were Henry Holland and John Nash, both involved with the Royal Pavilion, Brighton.

9. *Neo-Gothic* (later 19th century).
A Gothic revival, exemplified by the House of Commons (Sir Charles Barry and Augustus Welby Pugin), which imitated the medieval style.

10. *Art Nouveau* (1890s).
Style developed in France, characterized by sinuous lines and stylized flowers and foliage. It is represented in the work of Antonio Gaudi in Barcelona, Alfred Gilbert, and Charles Rennie Mackintosh, who designed the Glasgow School of Art.

11. *Art Deco* (1925-39).
Style originating in France which used heavy, geometric basic form, exemplified by the Radio City Music Hall in New York.

12. *Modernism* or *Functionism* (1901-80).
A style of architecture which attempted to exclude anything that lacked a purpose and sought to use the latest technological advances in the manufacture of concrete, steel and glass to full effect. Major exponents included Swiss born French architect Le Corbusier (Charles Édouard Jeanneret) who lived for many years in Marseille, devised town planning schemes for Marseille and Buenos Aires, and planned the purpose-built city of Brasilia. It also included Frank Lloyd Wright, who designed New York's Guggenheim Museum completed in 1959.

13. *Post Modernism* (1980s onwards).
High-tech architecture represented among others by Lord Richard Rogers, designer of Lloyd's building in London (1986) and previously co-designer of the Centre Pompidou in Paris (1977) with Renzo Piano.

British Architects

Inigo Jones (1573-1652)	–	Banqueting House, Whitehall/Cube Room, Wilton House/Queen's House at Greenwich/ Covent Garden (original square).
(Sir) Christopher Wren (1632-1723)	–	St. Paul's Cathedral/The Monument/Royal Chelsea Hospital/Greenwich Hospital.
(Sir) John Vanbrugh (1664-1726)	–	Blenheim Palace/Castle Howard.
Robert Adam (1728-1792)	–	Adelphi/Interiors of Harewood House, Osterley Park, Syon House, Kenwood House.
John Nash (1752-1835)	–	Buckingham Palace/Marble Arch/Regent St./Royal Pavilion (Brighton).
William Railton (1801-1877)	–	Nelson's Column.
(Sir) Charles Barry (1795-1860) } Augustus Welby Pugin (1812-1852) }	–	The Houses of Parliament.
(Sir) George Gilbert Scott (1811-1878)	–	St. Pancras Station/Albert Memorial.
Charles Rennie Mackintosh (1868-1928)	–	Glasgow School of Art.

(Sir) Edwin Lutyens (1869-1944)	–	Fountains in Trafalgar Square/The Cenotaph, Whitehall/Crypt of Metropolitan Cathedral (Liverpool)/Castle Drogo (Devon).
(Sir) Giles Gilbert Scott (1880-1960)	–	Anglican Cathedral (Liverpool)/Waterloo Bridge.
(Sir) Basil Spence (1907-1976)	–	Coventry Cathedral.
(Sir) Frederick Gibberd (1908-1984)	–	Metropolitan Cathedral (Liverpool)/ Harlow New Town.
(Sir) Denys Lasdun (1914-2001)	–	(Royal) National Theatre/Royal College of Physicians/University of East Anglia.
(Lord) Richard Rogers (1933-	–	Centre Pompidou (Paris)/Lloyd's building (London)/Millennium Dome.
(Lord) Norman Foster (1935-	–	Sainsbury Centre for Visual Arts (Norwich)/ Stansted Airport Terminal.
(Sir) Nicholas Grimshaw (1939-	–	Waterloo International Terminal/Eden Project (St. Austell, Cornwall).

British Engineers

Thomas Telford (1757-1834)	–	Menai Suspension Bridge.
Robert Stephenson (1803-1859)	–	Britannia Railway Bridge.
Isambard Kingdom Brunel (1806-1859)	–	Paddington and Temple Meads stations – Great Western Railway/Clifton Suspension Bridge/SS *Great Britain, Western* and *Eastern.*

PHILOSOPHY

Important Philosophers

Socrates (*c.* 470-399 BC)
Athenian-born Greek philosopher and intellectual leader who wrote nothing but features as the main character in the *Dialogues* of his pupil Plato, in which he searched for knowledge and truth using the Socratic method named after him. Charged with impiety and corrupting the youth of Athens, he was condemned by the authorities to commit suicide by drinking hemlock.

Plato (*c.* 427-347 BC)
Greek, pupil of Socrates and teacher of Aristotle, who founded a school at Athens called the Academy, where he taught philosophy and mathematics. His dialogues, of which about 30 survive, cover politics, ethics and metaphysics. The best known is the allegory, *The Republic,* which sets out the notion of Forms. Other dialogues include the *Symposium*, *Phaedo, Apology* and *Crito.*

Aristotle (384-322 BC)
Greek, born in Stagira, who studied in Athens under Plato before becoming personal tutor to Alexander the Great. He founded a school at Athens in a garden sacred to Apollo called the Lyceum. It became known as the peripatetic school from his custom of walking around the cloister as he lectured. His philosophy covered the whole realm of knowledge and his works include the *Nicomachean Ethics* and the *De Anima.*

St. Augustine of Hippo (354-430 AD)
Born in North Africa, of Roman descent, he was converted to Christianity and became one of the Fathers of the Church. His best known works are the *Confessions* and *The City of God.*

St. Thomas Aquinas (*c.* 1225-1274)
Italian-born Dominican friar known as the 'Angelic Doctor', who was the greatest exponent of the school of scholasticism. His philosophical system, known as Thomism, interpreted Aristotle according to Christian doctrine and became the basis of Catholic theology.

(Sir) Francis Bacon, Viscount St. Albans (1561-1626)
English philosopher, statesman and essayist who rejected Aristotelian deductive logic in favour of the inductive (Baconian) method, which stressed

that science advanced by empirical discovery. His works include *The Advancement of Learning, Novum Organum* and *The New Atlantis.*

Thomas Hobbes (1588-1679)
English political philosopher who argued in his major work *Leviathan* (1651) that absolutist government was the only way to ensure law and order.

René Descartes (1596-1650)
French mathematician and rationalist usually regarded as the founder of modern philosophy, and author of *Discourse on Method* (1637). The basis of Cartesian philosophy is expressed in his phrase *Cogito ergo sum* (I think, therefore I am).

Baruch (Benedict de) Spinoza (1632-1677)
Dutch rationalist philosopher who worked as a lens grinder in Amsterdam. His pantheistic view of the universe *(Deus sive Natura)* resulted in his excommunication from the Jewish faith, whereupon he changed his name from the Hebrew to the Latin for 'Blessed'. His main work the *Ethics* was published posthumously.

John Locke (1632-1704)
English founder of empiricism whose doctrine, expounded in his *Essay Concerning Human Understanding,* maintains that all knowledge is derived from experience. He believed that the mind at birth was a blank or *tabula rasa* and opposed the rationalist view that knowledge was derived from first principles.

Gottfried Wilhelm von Leibni(t)z (1646-1716)
German mathematician and rationalist philosopher who invented calculus independently of Newton. In *The Monadology* he argued that the world was composed of an infinite number of units called monads, the highest of which was God. His optimism ('this is the best of all possible worlds') was satirized in Voltaire's *Candide.*

Bishop George Berkeley (1685-1753)
Irish cleric who attempted to prove God's existence through his theory that the material world only exists when it is perceived by a mind. His dictum *esse est percipi* ('to exist is to be perceived') is set out in his *Essay towards a New Theory of Vision* and *A Treatise Concerning the Principles of Human Knowledge.*

David Hume (1711-1776)
Scottish historian and empirical philosopher who wrote *A Treatise of Human Nature* and *Dialogues Concerning Natural Religion.* He brought out the scepticism inherent in Locke's ideas.

Immanuel Kant (1724-1804)
German founder of critical philosophy whose *Critique of Pure Reason* argued that God's existence could not be proved theoretically. In ethics, he stated that right action conforms to a universal law based on reason which he called the *categorical imperative.*

Jeremy Bentham (1748-1832)
English philosopher, jurist and social reformer who founded utilitarianism. In *Principles of Morals and Legislation* (1789) he stated that society's aim should be 'the greatest happiness of the greatest number'.

Georg Wilhelm Friedrich Hegel (1770-1831)
German idealist philosopher. His dialectic method of reasoning involving a sequence of thesis, antithesis and synthesis proved difficult to comprehend. His doctrines influenced Karl Marx and led to modern totalitarianism.

Arthur Schopenhauer (1788-1860)
German anti-Hegelian follower of Kant, whose doctrine claimed that will is superior to knowledge. His chief work *The World as Will and ldea* expounds his pessimism and atheism.

John Stuart Mill (1806-1873)
English philosopher, economist and social reformer who ultimately modified some of Bentham's doctrines. His works include *A System of Logic, On Liberty, Utilitarianism* and *On the Subjection of Women,* in which he campaigned for female suffrage.

Sören Kierkegaard (1813-1855)
Danish founder of existentialism whose works include *Either-Or,* in which he opposed Hegel by asserting the importance of individual choice. Born in Copenhagen, the son of a Jewish merchant, he converted to Christianity. He stated that God could only be known through a 'leap of faith' rather than reason, and believed controversially that God and exceptional individuals were above moral laws.

Karl Marx (1818-1883)
German revolutionary thinker, born in Trier of Jewish parentage, who founded modern international Communism. With his life-long friend and collaborator, Friedrich Engels, he wrote *The Communist Manifesto* of 1848. Forced into exile, he settled in London in 1849 where he wrote *Das Kapital* (first volume published 1867). His massive tomb is in Highgate cemetery.

Friedrich Wilhelm Nietzsche (1844-1900)
German who rejected Christianity by arguing that 'God is dead'. His doctrine of the superman (*Übermensch*) expounded in *Thus Spake Zarathustra* and *Beyond Good and Evil* was later interpreted by Nazi ideologists as meaning 'Might is Right', so that he was seen as a precursor of Nazism.

Bertrand Russell (1872-1970)
English philosopher and mathematician, a noted agnostic and pacifist, who worked in the field of logic and adopted the view that scientific knowledge is the only factual knowledge (logical positivism). He wrote over sixty books including *Principia Mathematica* (with A.N. Whitehead), *The Problems of Philosophy* and *A History of Western Philosophy.*

Ludwig Wittgenstein (1889-1951)
Austrian linguistic philosopher, born in Vienna, who studied the nature and limits of language. His 'picture theory' expounded in *Tractatus Logico-Philosophicus* (1922) gave way to a quite different approach in his posthumously published *Philosophical Investigations.* He is considered the most influential figure in 20th century philosophy.

Jean-Paul Sartre (1905-1980)
Parisian-born French novelist, playwright and existentialist, a noted leftwing intellectual and atheist, whose major philosophical work was *L'Être et le Néant* (Being and Nothingness), which deals with human freedom.

(Sir) A(lfred) J(ules) Ayer (1910-1989)
English exponent of logical positivism, developed from Russell, whose works include *Language, Truth and Logic* (1936) and *The Problem of Knowledge* (1956).

Albert Camus (1913-1960)
Algerian-born French writer and existentialist, author of *The Plague, The Outsider* and the philosophical essay *The Myth of Sisyphus.* His writings often conflicted with other existentialist thinkers such as Sartre.

LITERATURE

Novelists

Author		*Major Works*
English		
John Bunyan (1628-1688)	–	Pilgrim's Progress (allegory written in Bedford gaol).
Samuel Richardson (1689-1761)	–	Pamela/Clarissa/Sir Charles Grandison (all epistolary novels).
Henry Fielding (1707-1754)	–	Joseph Andrews (a parody of Pamela)/ Tom Jones/Amelia.
Jane Austen (1775-1817) (wrote 6 novels)	–	Pride and Prejudice/Sense and Sensibility/ Emma/Persuasion/Northanger Abbey/ Mansfield Park.
William Makepeace Thackeray (1811-1863)	–	Vanity Fair (subtitled – A Novel Without a Hero)/Pendennis/The Virginians.
Charles Dickens (1812-1870) (wrote 15 novels)	–	David Copperfield/Oliver Twist/Great Expectations/Nicholas Nickleby/A Tale of Two Cities/Pickwick Papers/The Old Curiosity Shop/Hard Times/ Barnaby Rudge/Martin Chuzzlewit/ Bleak House/Little Dorrit/Dombey and Son/Our Mutual Friend/The Mystery of Edwin Drood (unfinished)/Christmas Stories (including A Christmas Carol).
Charlotte Brontë (1816-1855)	–	Jane Eyre/Shirley/Villette/The Professor.
Emily Brontë (1818-1848)	–	Wuthering Heights.
Anne Brontë (1820-1849)	–	The Tenant of Wildfell Hall/Agnes Grey.
Anthony Trollope (1815-1882)	–	The Barchester Chronicles (including The Warden, Barchester Towers and The Last Chronicle of Barset)/The Eustace Diamonds.
George Eliot (1819-1880)	–	Adam Bede/Mill on the Floss/Silas Marner/Middlemarch/Daniel Deronda.
George du Maurier (1834-1896)	–	Trilby.

Samuel Butler (1835-1902)	–	Erewhon (political satire)/The Way of All Flesh.
Thomas Hardy (1840-1928)	–	Far from the Madding Crowd/Tess of the D'Urbervilles/The Return of the Native/The Mayor of Casterbridge/Jude the Obscure/The Woodlanders/Under the Greenwood Tree/Wessex Tales/The Trumpet-Major/Two on a Tower/A Pair of Blue Eyes/The Well-Beloved/Desperate Remedies/The Dynasts (epic drama).
Joseph Conrad (1857-1924)	–	Almayer's Folly/An Outcast of the Islands/Lord Jim/Nostromo/Mirror of the Sea/The Secret Agent/Under Western Eyes/The Rescue/Youth; Heart of Darkness; Typhoon; The End of the Tether (short stories).
(Sir) Anthony Hope (Hawkins) (1863-1933)	–	The Prisoner of Zenda/Rupert of Hentzau.
(Enoch) Arnold Bennett (1867-1931)	–	Anna of the Five Towns/The Old Wives' Tale/Clayhanger series (trilogy)/ The Card.
John Galsworthy (1867-1933)	–	The Man of Property/In Chancery/To Let (The Forsyte Saga).
W(illiam) Somerset Maugham (1874-1965)	–	Liza of Lambeth/Of Human Bondage/ The Moon and Sixpence/Cakes and Ale/ The Painted Veil/The Razor's Edge/The Circle; The Constant Wife; For Services Rendered; Home and Beauty (plays).
Flora Thompson (1876-1947)	–	Lark Rise to Candleford (trilogy).
E(dward) M(organ) Forster (1879-1970)	–	Where Angels Fear to Tread/A Room with a View/Howard's End/A Passage to India/Maurice/The Longest Journey.
Virginia Woolf (1882-1941)	–	The Voyage Out/Jacob's Room/Mrs Dalloway/To the Lighthouse/Orlando/The Waves/The Years/A Room of One's Own.
D(avid) H(erbert) Lawrence (1885-1930)	–	Lady Chatterley's Lover/Women in Love/ Sons and Lovers/The Rainbow/The White Peacock/The Fox/The Virgin and the Gypsy/Love Among the Haystacks/ Aaron's Rod/Kangaroo/The Plumed Serpent.

C(ecil) S(cott) Forester (1899-1966)	–	Horatio Hornblower series/The African Queen/The Earthly Paradise/ Payment Deferred/Brown on Resolution.
George Orwell (1903-1950)	–	Animal Farm/1984/Down and Out in Paris and London/Burmese Days/ Homage to Catalonia/Keep the Aspidistra Flying/Coming Up for Air/ The Road to Wigan Pier.
Evelyn Waugh (1903-1966)	–	Brideshead Revisited/A Handful of Dust/Decline and Fall/Scoop/The Loved One/Black Mischief/Men at Arms/Officers and Gentlemen.
(Henry) Graham Greene (1904-1991)	–	Stamboul Train/Brighton Rock/The Power and the Glory/The Heart of the Matter/The Third Man/The End of the Affair/The Quiet American/Our Man in Havana/A Burnt-out Case/The Comedians/Travels with My Aunt/ The Honorary Consul/The Living Room (play)/The Potting Shed (play).
Anthony Powell (1905-2000)	–	A Dance to the Music of Time/The Fisher King.
Daphne du Maurier (1907-1991)	–	Rebecca/My Cousin Rachel/Jamaica Inn/Frenchman's Creek.
(Sir) William Golding (1911-1993)	–	Lord of the Flies/Rites of Passage/The Spire/Pincher Martin.
Lawrence Durrell (1912-1990)	–	The Alexandria Quartet: Justine; Balthazar; Mountolive; Clea.
Anthony Burgess (1917-1993)	–	A Clockwork Orange/Earthly Powers/ 1985/The Pianoplayers.
Salman Rushdie (1947- (Indian born)	–	Midnight's Children/Shame/The Satanic Verses.

Scottish

(Sir) Walter Scott (1771-1832)	–	Waverley/Guy Mannering/Old Mortality/Rob Roy/The Heart of Midlothian/The Bride of Lammermoor/A Legend of Montrose/Ivanhoe/Kenilworth/The Fortunes of Nigel/Peveril of the Peak/Quentin Durward/Redgauntlet/The Betrothed/The Talisman/Woodstock/St. Valentine's Day or the Fair Maid of Perth.

Irish

James Joyce (1882-1941)	–	Ulysses/Finnegan's Wake/A Portrait of the Artist as a Young Man.
(Dame) Iris Murdoch (1919-1999)	–	A Severed Head/The Black Prince/The Sea, the Sea/The Sandcastle/The Bell/The Philosopher's Pupil/The Message to the Planet/The Book and the Brotherhood.

French

Voltaire (1694-1778)	–	Candide/Zadig (satirical short story).
Stendhal (1783-1842)	–	Le Rouge et le Noir (Scarlet and Black)/La Chartreuse de Parme (the Charterhouse of Parma).
Honoré de Balzac (1799-1850)	–	La Comédie Humaine (the Human Comedy) including Eugénie Grandet and Le Père Goriot (Old Goriot).
Alexandre Dumas (père) (1802-1870)	–	The Three Musketeers/The Count of Monte Cristo.
Victor Hugo (1802-1885)	–	The Hunchback of Notre Dame/Les Misérables.
Gustave Flaubert (1821-1880)	–	Madame Bovary/Sentimental Education.
Émile Zola (1840-1902)	–	Thérèse Raquin/the Rougon-Macquart series including Nana and Germinal.
André Gide (1869-1951)	–	La Porte Étroite/La Symphonie Pastorale/Les Faux-Monnayeurs (the Counterfeiters).
Marcel Proust (1871-1922)	–	À la Recherche du Temps Perdu (Remembrance of Things Past).

Jean-Paul Sartre (1905-1980)	–	Les Chemins de la Liberté (Roads to Freedom)/play – Huis Clos (In Camera).
Albert Camus (1913-1960)	–	L'Étranger (The Outsider)/La Peste (The Plague)/L'Homme Révolté (The Rebel).
German		
Heinrich Mann (1871-1950)	–	Professor Unrat (The Blue Angel).
Thomas Mann (1875-1955)	–	Buddenbrooks/Der Zauberberg (The Magic Mountain)/Confessions of Felix Krull/Tonio Kröger (short story)/Der Tod in Venedig (Death in Venice) – (short story).
Erich Maria Remarque (1898-1970)	–	All Quiet on the Western Front.
Günter Grass (1927-	–	Die Blechtrommel (The Tin Drum).
Italian		
Giovanni Boccaccio (1313-1375)	–	The Decameron (100 tales).
Spanish		
Miguel de Saavedra Cervantes (1547-1616)	–	Don Quixote (de la Mancha).
Russian		
Alexander Pushkin (1799-1837)	–	Eugene Onegin (novel in verse)/Boris Godunov (drama)/The Queen of Spades/ The Captain's Daughter.
Ivan Turgenev (1818-1883)	–	A Month in the Country/Fathers and Sons.
Fyodor Dostoevsky (1821-1881)	–	Crime and Punishment/The Brothers Karamazov/The Idiot/The Gambler/ The Possessed.
(Count) Leo Tolstoy (1828-1910)	–	War and Peace/Anna Karenina.
Maxim Gorky (1868-1936)	–	My Childhood/My Universities/In the World/Twenty-Six Men and a Girl/The Mother.
Boris Pasternak (1890-1960)	–	Dr Zhivago.
Vladimir Nabokov (1899-1977)	–	Lolita.

Mikhail Sholokhov (1905-1984)	–	And Quiet Flows the Don.
Alexander Solzhenitsyn (1918-	–	One Day in the Life of Ivan Denisovich/The First Circle/Cancer Ward/The Gulag Archipelago.

American

Herman Melville (1819-1891)	–	Moby Dick.
Henry James (1843-1916)	–	The American/Daisy Miller/Portrait of a Lady/Washington Square (play – The Heiress)/The Bostonians/The Ambassadors/The Wings of the Dove/The Golden Bowl/The Turn of the Screw (ghost story, became play The Innocents)/ The Aspern Papers.
F(rancis) Scott Fitzgerald (1896-1940)	–	The Great Gatsby/Tender Is the Night/The Last Tycoon (unfinished).
William Faulkner (1897-1962)	–	The Sound and the Fury/As I Lay Dying/ Sanctuary/Light in August/Absalom, Absalom!/The Unvanquished/The Hamlet (filmed as The Long Hot Summer)/ Intruder in the Dust/Requiem for a Nun/ A Fable/The Town/The Mansion.
Ernest Hemingway (1899-1961)	–	The Sun Also Rises/A Farewell to Arms/ Death in the Afternoon/The Green Hills of Africa/For Whom the Bell Tolls/The Old Man and the Sea.
Margaret Mitchell (1900-1949)	–	Gone with the Wind.
John Steinbeck (1902-1968)	–	Of Mice and Men/The Grapes of Wrath/Cannery Row/East of Eden.
J(erome) D(avid) Salinger (1919-	–	The Catcher in the Rye.
Norman Mailer (1923-	–	The Naked and the Dead/An American Dream/The Executioner's Song.
Truman Capote (1924-1984)	–	Other Voices, Other Rooms/Breakfast at Tiffany's/In Cold Blood.
Ira Levin (1929-	–	A Kiss Before Dying/Rosemary's Baby/ The Stepford Wives/The Boys from Brazil/Sliver/Deathtrap (play)/Veronica's Room (play).

Children's Literature

Author		*Best Sellers*
Louisa May Alcott	–	Little Women/Good Wives/Jo's Boys/ Little Men.
R(obert) M(ichael) Ballantyne	–	The Coral Island.
R(ichard) D(oddridge) Blackmore	–	Lorna Doone.
Enid Blyton	–	The Famous Five stories/The Secret Seven stories/Noddy stories.
Raymond Briggs	–	The Snowman/Father Christmas/Granpa/ When the Wind Blows.
John Buchan (Baron Tweedsmuir)	–	The Thirty-Nine Steps/The Power House/Greenmantle/Prester John/The Three Hostages.
Frances Hodgson Burnett	–	Little Lord Fauntleroy/The Secret Garden/A Little Princess.
Edgar Rice Burroughs	–	Tarzan of the Apes stories.
Lewis Carroll	–	Alice's Adventures in Wonderland/ Through the Looking Glass/The Hunting of the Snark/Jabberwocky.
Susan Coolidge	–	What Katy Did/What Katy Did at School/What Katy Did Next.
James Fenimore Cooper	–	The Last of the Mohicans.
Richmal Crompton	–	William stories.
Roald Dahl	–	Charlie and the Chocolate Factory/ James and the Giant Peach/Fantastic Mr Fox/The Witches/Matilda/George's Marvellous Medicine.
Daniel Defoe	–	Robinson Crusoe.
Ian Fleming (creator of James Bond)	–	Chitty Chitty Bang Bang.
Paul Gallico	–	The Snow Goose/Jenny.
Kenneth Grahame	–	The Wind in the Willows.
(Sir) H(enry) Rider Haggard	–	King Solomon's Mines/She/Allan Quatermain.
Thomas Hughes	–	Tom Brown's Schooldays.
Capt. W(illiam) E(arl) Johns	–	Biggles, Gimlet and Worralls stories.
Charles Kingsley	–	The Water Babies.
Rudyard Kipling	–	The Jungle Book/The Second Jungle Book/Captains Courageous/Stalky and Co/Kim/Just So Stories/Puck of Pook's Hill/Rewards and Fairies.

Laurie Lee	–	Cider with Rosie.
C(live) S(taples) Lewis	–	The Narnia Chronicles (The Lion, the Witch and the Wardrobe etc.).
Jack London	–	Call of the Wild/White Fang.
Frederick Marryat ('Captain Marryat')	–	Peter Simple/Mr Midshipman Easy/ Masterman Ready/Children of the New Forest.
A(lan) A(lexander) Milne	–	Winnie-the-Pooh/The House at Pooh Corner.
L(ucy) M(aud) Montgomery	–	Anne of Green Gables.
E(dith) Nesbit	–	The Railway Children/The Treasure-Seekers.
Eleanor Porter	–	Pollyanna.
Beatrix Potter	–	The Tale of Peter Rabbit.
Arthur Ransome	–	Swallows and Amazons.
Frank Richards	–	Billy Bunter stories.
J(oanne) K(athleen) Rowling	–	Harry Potter and the Philosopher's Stone/ Harry Potter and the Chamber of Secrets/ Harry Potter and the Prisoner of Azkaban/ Harry Potter and the Goblet of Fire/Harry Potter and the Order of the Phoenix.
Anna Sewell	–	Black Beauty.
Johanna Spyri	–	Heidi.
Robert Louis Stevenson	–	Treasure Island/Kidnapped/Catriona/ The Master of Ballantrae/Dr Jekyll and Mr Hyde.
Harriet Beecher Stowe	–	Uncle Tom's Cabin.
Jonathan Dean Swift	–	Gulliver's Travels.
J(ohn) R(onald) R(euel) Tolkien	–	The Hobbit/The Lord of the Rings.
Sue Townsend	–	The Secret Diary of Adrian Mole.
P(amela) L(yndon) Travers	–	Mary Poppins.
Mark Twain	–	Tom Sawyer/Huckleberry Finn.
Johann Wyss	–	Swiss Family Robinson.

Horror Story Writers

Horace Walpole	–	The Castle of Otranto.
Mary Shelley	–	Frankenstein.
Bram Stoker	–	Dracula.
Stephen King	–	Carrie/'Salem's Lot/The Shining/Cujo/ Christine/The Dead Zone/Creepshow/ Cat's Eyes/Pet Sematary/Misery/Needful Things/Gerald's Game/Dolores Claiborne.
James Herbert	–	The Rats/The Fog.

Detective Story Writers

Edgar Allan Poe	–	Murders in the Rue Morgue (first detective story – 1841).
William Wilkie Collins	–	The Woman in White (first English detective novel – 1860)/The Moonstone.
(Sir) Arthur Conan Doyle	–	Sherlock Holmes stories.
G(ilbert) K(eith) Chesterton	–	Father Brown stories.
Agatha Christie	–	Hercule Poirot stories/Miss Marple stories.
Dorothy L(eigh) Sayers	–	Lord Peter Wimsey stories, e.g. The Nine Tailors/Busman's Honeymoon.
Dashiell Hammett	–	The Maltese Falcon/The Thin Man/ The Glass Key.
Raymond Chandler	–	The Big Sleep/Farewell My Lovely.
Erle Stanley Gardner	–	Perry Mason stories.
Georges Simenon	–	Inspector Maigret stories.
Colin Dexter	–	Inspector Morse stories.
Ruth Rendell	–	Chief Inspector Wexford stories.
P(hyllis) D(orothy) James	–	Superintendent Adam Dalgliesh stories.
Ian Rankin	–	Inspector Rebus stories.

Science Fiction Writers

Isaac Asimov	–	Foundation series/Nemesis.
(Sir) Arthur C(harles) Clarke	–	Childhood's End/2001 – A Space Odyssey/2010 Space Odyssey II/2061 Space Odyssey III/Rendezvous with Rama/Rama II.
Frank Herbert	–	Dune series.
Jules Verne	–	20,000 Leagues under the Sea/A Journey to the Centre of the Earth/ From Earth to Moon/Round the Moon/ Around the World in Eighty Days.
H(erbert) G(eorge) Wells	–	The Time Machine/The Invisible Man/ The War of the Worlds/The First Men in the Moon/The Shape of Things to Come/ The Sleeper Awakes/The Food of the Gods/The War in the Air.

Poets

Poet		*Well Known Poems/Volumes*
English		
Geoffrey Chaucer (*c.*1343-1400)	–	The Canterbury Tales (narrative poem).
Edmund Spenser (1552-1599)	–	The Faerie Queene (allegory).
John Donne (1572-1631)	–	Sonnets (e.g. Death be not Proud).
Robert Herrick (1591-1674)	–	To the Virgins, to Make Much of Time/ Cherry-ripe.
John Milton (1608-1674)	–	Paradise Lost/Paradise Regained/Samson Agonistes/Il Penseroso/Comus/Lycidas/ On His Blindness.
John Dryden (1631-1700)	–	Annus Mirabilis/Absalom and Achitophel/ Ode on St. Cecilia's Day.
Thomas Gray (1716-1771)	–	Elegy Written in a Country Churchyard.
William Cowper (1731-1800)	–	John Gilpin/The Task.
George Crabbe (1754-1832)	–	The Village/The Borough.
William Blake (1757-1827)	–	Songs of Innocence and Experience (inc. The Tyger)/Jerusalem.
William Wordsworth (1770-1850)	–	Daffodils/My Heart Leaps Up/Tintern Abbey/Upon Westminster Bridge/Ode: Intimations of Immortality/Ode to Duty/ The Prelude.
Samuel Taylor Coleridge (1772-1834)	–	The Rime of the Ancient Mariner/ Kubla Khan/Christabel.
Robert Southey (1774-1843)	–	The Battle of Blenheim/The Inchcape Rock/Bishop Hatto/The Old Man's Comforts/Bishop Bruno.
James Leigh Hunt (1784-1859)	–	Abou Ben Adhem/The Nile.
Rev. R(ichard) H(arris) Barham (1788-1845)	–	The Jackdaw of Rheims/The Ingoldsby Legends.

George Gordon, Lord Byron (1788-1824)	–	Childe Harold's Pilgrimage/The Prisoner of Chillon/Don Juan/The Destruction of Sennacherib.
Percy Bysshe Shelley (1792-1822)	–	To a Skylark/Ode to the West Wind/ Adonais.
John Keats (1795-1821)	–	Endymion/The Eve of St. Agnes/Ode to a Nightingale/Ode on a Grecian Urn/To Autumn/La Belle Dame Sans Merci/On First Looking into Chapman's Homer.
Elizabeth Barrett Browning (1806-1861)	–	The Cry of the Children/Sonnets from the Portuguese/Aurora Leigh.
Alfred, Lord Tennyson (1809-1892)	–	The Charge of the Light Brigade/The Lady of Shalott/The Revenge/The Princess/In Memoriam/Maud/Idylls of the King.
Robert Browning (1812-1889)	–	The Pied Piper of Hamelin/How They Brought the Good News from Ghent to Aix/Pippa Passes/Home-Thoughts, from Abroad/Home-Thoughts, from the Sea/Rabbi Ben Ezra.
Robert Bridges (1844-1930)	–	London Snow/The Testament of Beauty.
A(lfred) E(dward) Housman (1859-1936)	–	A Shropshire Lad.
Laurence Binyon (1869-1943)	–	For the Fallen/Tristram's End.
William Henry Davies (1871-1940)	–	Leisure/Money/School's Out.
Walter de la Mare (1873-1956)	–	The Listeners/Silver.
John Masefield (1878-1967)	–	Cargoes/Sea-fever.
James Elroy Flecker (1884-1915)	–	The Golden Journey to Samarkand/The Bridge of Fire/Old Ships.
Siegfried Sassoon (1886-1967)	–	Attack/Everyone Sang.
Rupert (Chawner) Brooke (1887-1915)	–	The Soldier/The Old Vicarage, Grantchester.
Wilfred Owen (1893-1918)	–	Dulce et Decorum Est/Anthem for Doomed Youth/Disabled.

Stevie Smith (1902-1971)	–	Not Waving but Drowning.
(Sir) John Betjeman (1906-1984)	–	A Subaltern's Love-song/The Metropolitan Railway/Summoned by Bells.
W(ystan) H(ugh) Auden (1907-1973)	–	In Memory of W.B.Yeats/The Night Mail/Miss Gee.
Philip Larkin (1922-1985)	–	The North Ship/The Whitsun Weddings/High Windows.
Ted Hughes (1930-1998)	–	The Hawk in the Rain/Wodwo/Crow.

Scottish

Robert Burns (1759-1796)	–	Tam O'Shanter/To a Mouse/Auld Lang Syne/Comin' Through the Rye.

Irish

W(illiam) B(utler) Yeats (1865-1939)	–	The Lake Isle of Innisfree/An Irish Airman Foresees His Death.
Cecil Day Lewis (1904-1972)	–	Overtures to Death.

American

Ralph Waldo Emerson (1803-1882)	–	Give All to Love/Brahma/The Problem.
Henry Wadsworth Longfellow (1807-1882)	–	The Song of Hiawatha/Excelsior/The Village Blacksmith/The Wreck of the Hesperus/Paul Revere's Ride.
Edgar Allan Poe (1809-1849)	–	The Raven/The Bells/Annabel Lee/Lenore.
Walt Whitman (1819-1892)	–	O Captain! My Captain!/Song of Myself/Reconciliation.
Emily Dickinson (1830-1886)	–	Parting/A Bird Came Down the Walk.
Robert Frost (1874-1963)	–	Stopping by Woods on a Snowy Evening/The Gift Outright.
Ezra Pound (1885-1972)	–	Cantos/Hugh Selwyn Mauberley.
Ogden Nash (1902-1971)	–	I'm a Stranger Here Myself/Versus/Bed Riddance.
Sylvia Plath (1932-1963)	–	The Colossus/Ariel.

French

Alphonse de Lamartine (1790-1869)	–	Méditations inc. Le Lac.
Alfred de Musset (1810-1857)	–	Le Saule (The Willow).
Charles Baudelaire (1821-1867)	–	Les Fleurs du mal (Flowers of Evil).

Italian

Dante Alighieri (1265-1321)	–	La divina commedia (The Divine Comedy).

Greek

Homer (*c.* 8th century BC)	–	Iliad/Odyssey.

Roman

Virgil (70 -19 BC)	–	Aeneid/Eclogues (Bucolics)/Georgics.
Ovid (43 BC -17 AD)	–	The Art of Love/Metamorphoses.

Literary Pseudonyms

Author		*Nom-de-Plume (Pen-name)*
Jean Baptiste Poquelin (1622-73)	–	Molière.
François-Marie Arouet (1694-1778)	–	Voltaire.
Charles Lamb (1775-1834)	–	Elia.
Marie-Henri Beyle (1783-1842)	–	Stendhal.
Amandine-Aurore Lucil(l)e Dupin, Baronne Dudevant (1804-76)	–	George Sand.
Charles Dickens (1812-70)	–	Boz.
Charlotte Brontë (1816-55)	–	Currer Bell.
Emily Brontë (1818-48)	–	Ellis Bell.
Anne Brontë (1820-49)	–	Acton Bell.
Mary Ann Evans (1819-80)	–	George Eliot.
Charles Lutwidge Dodgson (1832-98)	–	Lewis Carroll.
Samuel Langhorne Clemens (1835-1910)	–	Mark Twain.
Teodor Jozef Konrad Korzeniowski (1857-1924)	–	Joseph Conrad.
William Sydney Porter (1862-1910)	–	O. Henry.
(Sir) Arthur Quiller-Couch (1863-1944)	–	Q.
Alexei Peshkov (1868-1936)	–	Maxim Gorky.
Hector Hugh Munro (1870-1916)	–	Saki.
John Griffith (1876-1916)	–	Jack London.
H(erman) C(yril) McNeile (1888-1937)	–	Sapper.
Eric Arthur Blair (1903-50)	–	George Orwell.
Cecil Day Lewis (1904-72)	–	Nicholas Blake.
Harry Patterson (1929-	–	Jack Higgins.
David John Cornwell (1931-	–	John Le Carré.
Ruth Rendell (1932-	–	Barbara Vine.
Ian Rankin (1960-	–	Jack Harvey.

THE THEATRE

Some Theatres of the British Isles

London	–	Adelphi/Albery/Aldwych/Apollo (Shaftesbury Avenue)/Apollo Victoria/Arts/Barbican Theatre and Pit/Cambridge/Coliseum/Comedy/Criterion/Dominion/Donmar Warehouse/Drury Lane, Theatre Royal/Duchess/Duke of York's/Fortune/Garrick/Gielgud/Greenwich/Haymarket, Theatre Royal/Her Majesty's/Lilian Baylis/London Palladium/Lyceum/Lyric (Shaftesbury Avenue)/Lyric, Hammersmith/Mayfair/Mermaid/(Royal) National Theatre – Olivier; Lyttelton; Cottesloe/New Ambassadors/New London, Drury Lane/Old Vic/Open Air Theatre, Regent's Park/Palace/Peacock/Phoenix/Piccadilly/Players Theatre/The Playhouse/Prince Edward/Prince of Wales/Queen's/Richmond/Royal Court/Royal Opera House, Covent Garden/Sadler's Wells/St.Martin's/Savoy/Shaftesbury/Shakespeare's Globe/Strand/Theatre Royal, Stratford East/Vaudeville/Victoria Palace/Westminster/Whitehall/Wimbledon/Wyndham's/Young Vic.
London Fringe	–	Almeida/Bloomsbury/Bush/Cochrane/Gate/Half Moon/Hampstead Theatre Club/Jermyn St./King's Head/New End, Hampstead Village/Old Red Lion/Orange Tree, Richmond/Pleasance/Riverside Studios/Soho/Tricycle.
Aberdeen	–	His Majesty's/Capitol.
Bath	–	Theatre Royal.
Belfast	–	Lyric Players/Grand Opera House.
Bexhill-on-Sea	–	De La Warr Pavilion.
Birmingham	–	Alexandra/Rep/Hippodrome.
Blackpool	–	Grand/Opera House.
Bolton	–	Octagon.

Bournemouth	–	Pavilion.
Bradford	–	Alhambra.
Brighton	–	Theatre Royal/Dome/Gardner Arts Centre/ Komedia.
Bristol	–	Old Vic/Hippodrome/Theatre Royal.
Bromley	–	Churchill.
Bury St. Edmunds	–	Theatre Royal.
Buxton	–	Opera House.
Cambridge	–	Arts Theatre.
Canterbury	–	Marlowe.
Cardiff	–	New/Sherman.
Cheltenham	–	Everyman.
Chester	–	Gateway.
Chesterfield	–	Pomegranate.
Chichester	–	Festival Theatre/Minerva Studio.
Colchester	–	Mercury.
Coventry	–	Belgrade/Warwick Arts Centre.
Crawley	–	The Hawth.
Croydon	–	Ashcroft/Warehouse.
Derby	–	Playhouse.
Dublin	–	Abbey/Gate/Peacock/Gaiety.
Eastbourne	–	Congress/Devonshire Park/Winter Garden.
Edinburgh	–	King's/Lyceum/Traverse.
Exeter	–	Northcott.
Glasgow	–	Citizens'/King's/Pavilion/Tramway/Tron.
Guildford	–	Yvonne Arnaud.
Hastings	–	White Rock/The Stables.
Hornchurch	–	Queen's.
Hull	–	New/Spring Street.
Ipswich	–	New Wolsey.
Lancaster	–	Dukes Playhouse.
Leeds	–	West Yorkshire Playhouse/Grand/Civic.
Leicester	–	Haymarket/Phoenix.
Liverpool	–	Playhouse/Everyman/Empire.
Manchester	–	Royal Exchange/Contact/Forum/Library.
Newbury	–	Watermill.
Newcastle-under-Lyme	–	New Victoria.
Newcastle-upon-Tyne	–	Theatre Royal/Playhouse.
Norwich	–	Theatre Royal.

Nottingham	–	Playhouse/Theatre Royal.
Oldham	–	Coliseum.
Oxford	–	Playhouse/Apollo/Old Fire Station.
Peterborough	–	Key.
Plymouth	–	Mayflower/Drum/Theatre Royal.
Portsmouth	–	New Theatre Royal.
Reading	–	Hexagon/The Mill At Sonning.
Salisbury	–	Playhouse.
Scarborough	–	Stephen Joseph/Futurist/Spa.
Sheffield	–	Crucible/Lyceum.
Southampton	–	Mayflower/Nuffield.
Southsea	–	King's Theatre.
Stratford-Upon-Avon	–	Royal Shakespeare Theatre/Swan/ The Other Place.
Swindon	–	Wyvern.
Torquay	–	Princess.
Wakefield	–	Theatre Royal.
Watford	–	Palace.
Winchester	–	Theatre Royal.
Windsor	–	Theatre Royal.
Woking	–	New Victoria.
Wolverhampton	–	Grand/Arena.
Worcester	–	Swan.
Worthing	–	Connaught/Pavilion.
York	–	Theatre Royal/Grand Opera House.

Dramatists

Author		*Major Works*
English		
Christopher Marlowe (1564-1593)	–	(The Tragical History of) Dr Faustus/ Edward II/The Jew of Malta/Tamburlaine the Great.
William Shakespeare (1564-1616) (wrote 37 plays)	–	Hamlet/Macbeth/Othello/King Lear/Romeo and Juliet/Julius Caesar/A Midsummer Night's Dream/The Merchant of Venice/The Taming of the Shrew/Much Ado About Nothing/As You Like It/Twelfth Night/ Cymbeline/The Winter's Tale/The Tempest/ The Comedy of Errors/Henry IV (parts 1

		and 2)/Henry V/Henry VI (parts 1, 2 and 3)/ Richard II/Richard III/Antony and Cleopatra/Coriolanus/The Two Gentlemen of Verona/The Merry Wives of Windsor/ Measure for Measure/Love's Labour's Lost/ All's Well That Ends Well/King John/Henry VIII/Troilus and Cressida/Titus Andronicus/ Timon of Athens/Pericles, Prince of Tyre. (NB. Hamlet – longest play; The Comedy of Errors – shortest play).
Thomas Middleton (*c.* 1570-1627) and William Rowley (*c.* 1585-*c.* 1642)	–	The Changeling.
Ben(jamin) Jonson (1572-1637)	–	Volpone, or the Fox/The Alchemist/ Bartholomew Fair/Every Man in His Humour/Every Man out of His Humour.
John Webster (1580-1634)	–	The White Devil/The Duchess of Malfi.
John Ford (1586-1640)	–	'Tis Pity She's a Whore/The Broken Heart.
(Sir) George Etherege (*c.* 1635-1692)	–	The Man of Mode/The Comical Revenge, or Love in a Tub.
Aphra Behn (1640-1689)	–	The Rover.
William Wycherley (1640-1716)	–	The Country Wife/The Plain Dealer.
(Sir) John Vanbrugh (1664-1726)	–	The Relapse, or Virtue in Danger/The Provok'd Wife.
William Congreve (1670-1729)	–	The Way of the World/The Double Dealer/Love for Love/The Old Bachelor/ The Mourning Bride.
Richard Brinsley Sheridan (1751-1816) (Anglo-Irish; born Dublin)	–	The Rivals/The School for Scandal/The Critic.
(Sir) Arthur Wing Pinero (1855-1934)	–	The Magistrate/The Schoolmistress/ Dandy Dick/The Second Mrs Tanqueray/ Trelawny of the 'Wells'/The Cabinet Minister/The Gay Lord Quex.
Harley Granville-Barker (1877-1946)	–	The Voysey Inheritance/Waste/The Madras House/The Secret Life.

Frederick Lonsdale (1881-1954)	–	The Last of Mrs Cheyney/On Approval/ Aren't We All?/Canaries Sometimes Sing.
T(homas) S(tearns) Eliot (1888-1965) (American born; British subject from 1927)	–	Murder in the Cathedral/The Family Reunion/The Cocktail Party/The Waste Land; Old Possum's Book of Practical Cats; Four Quartets; Ash Wednesday (poems).
J(ohn) B(oynton) Priestley (1894-1984)	–	An Inspector Calls/Dangerous Corner/ Time and the Conways/I Have Been Here Before/The Linden Tree/When We Are Married/The Good Companions (novel)/ Angel Pavement (novel).
R(obert) C(edric) Sherriff (1896-1975)	–	Journey's End/Home at Seven.
(Sir) Noël Coward (1899-1973)	–	The Vortex/Hay Fever/Private Lives/ Cavalcade/Design for Living/Blithe Spirit/Bitter Sweet/Present Laughter/ Still Life (filmed as Brief Encounter)/ Easy Virtue/Peace in Our Time/Post Mortem/Fallen Angels/Relative Values/A Song at Twilight/Semi-Monde/Star Quality.
Patrick Hamilton (1904-1962)	–	Gaslight/Rope/The West Pier/Hangover Square; The Gorse Trilogy; The Slaves of Solitude (novels).
Christopher Fry (1907-	–	The Lady's Not for Burning/Venus Observed/A Sleep of Prisoners.
Bill Naughton (1910-1992)	–	All in Good Time (filmed as The Family Way)/Alfie/Spring and Port Wine.
(Sir) Terence Rattigan (1911-1977)	–	The Browning Version/The Winslow Boy/Separate Tables/The Deep Blue Sea/In Praise of Love/Cause Célèbre/ Flare Path/French Without Tears/Ross/ Harlequinade.
James Saunders (1925-	–	Next Time I'll Sing to You/A Scent of Flowers/Bodies/Making It Better/Retreat.
Anthony Shaffer (1926-2001)	–	Sleuth/Murderer/The Case of the Oily Levantine (Whodunnit).
(Sir) Peter Shaffer (1926-	–	The Royal Hunt of the Sun/Equus/ Amadeus/Five Finger Exercise/Black Comedy/ The Private Ear and The Public Eye/Lettice and Lovage/Yonadab/The Gift of the Gorgon.

Peter Nichols (1927-	–	A Day in the Death of Joe Egg/The National Health/Forget-Me-Not Lane/Chez Nous/Born in the Gardens/Privates on Parade/Passion Play/Poppy.
John Osborne (1929-1994)	–	Look Back in Anger/The Entertainer/ Luther/Inadmissible Evidence/A Patriot for Me/Hotel in Amsterdam/West of Suez/Déjàvu.
Harold Pinter (1930-	–	The Birthday Party/The Caretaker/ The Homecoming/Betrayal/Other Places/ No Man's Land/Moonlight/The Hothouse.
Peter Whelan (1931-	–	The Accrington Pals/Clay/The School of Night/Shakespeare Country/The Herbal Bed/A Russian in the Woods.
Arnold Wesker (1932-	–	Chicken Soup with Barley; Roots; I'm Talking About Jerusalem (trilogy)/ Chips with Everything/The Kitchen.
Joe Orton (1933-1967)	–	Entertaining Mr Sloane/Loot/The Erpingham Camp/What the Butler Saw.
Michael Frayn (1933-	–	The Two of Us/Alphabetical Order/ Donkeys' Years/Make and Break/Noises Off/Benefactors/Here/Copenhagen/Alarms and Excursions/Democracy.
David Storey (1933-	–	In Celebration/Early Days/Home/The Contractor/The Changing Room/ Cromwell/Life Class/Mother's Day/ Sisters/Jubilee (The March on Russia)/ Stages/This Sporting Life (novel).
Alan Bennett (1934-	–	Beyond the Fringe/Forty Years On/ Getting On/Habeas Corpus/The Old Country/Single Spies: An Englishman Abroad and A Question of Attribution/ Talking Heads/The Madness of George III/The Lady in the Van/Office Suite.
Richard Harris (1934-	–	Outside Edge/Stepping Out/The Business of Murder/The Maintenance Man/Dead Guilty.
Ronald Harwood (1934- (born in South Africa)	–	The Dresser/Another Time/Taking Sides/ The Handyman/Equally Divided/Quartet/ Mahler's Conversion.

Hugh Whitemore (1936-	–	Stevie/Pack of Lies (Act of Betrayal – TV)/Breaking the Code/The Best of Friends/It's Ralph/God Only Knows.
Simon Gray (1937-	–	Butley/Otherwise Engaged/The Rear Column/Stage Struck/Quartermaine's Terms/ The Common Pursuit/Melon/Hidden Laughter/Cell Mates/Simply Disconnected/ Life Support/Japes/The Holy Terror.
(Sir) Tom Stoppard (1937- (born in Czechoslovakia)	–	Enter a Free Man/Rosencrantz and Guildenstern Are Dead/The Real Inspector Hound/Jumpers/Travesties/Dirty Linen/ Every Good Boy Deserves Favour/ Professional Foul (TV)/Night and Day/ The Real Thing/On the Razzle/Dalliance/ Rough Crossing/Arcadia/Indian Ink/The Invention of Love/The Coast of Utopia: Voyage; Shipwreck; Salvage.
Caryl Churchill (1938-	–	Cloud Nine/Top Girls/Serious Money/ Icecream/Light Shining in Buckinghamshire/Far Away/A Number.
Tom Kempinski (1938-	–	Duet for One/Separation.
(Sir) Alan Ayckbourn (1939-	–	Relatively Speaking/How the Other Half Loves/Family Circles/Time and Time Again/Absurd Person Singular/The Norman Conquests: Table Manners; Living Together; Round and Round the Garden/ Absent Friends/Confusions/ Bedroom Farce/Just Between Ourselves/ Ten Times Table/Joking Apart/Sisterly Feelings/ Taking Steps/Season's Greetings/Way Upstream/Intimate Exchanges/It Could Be Any One of Us/A Chorus of Disapproval/ Woman in Mind/A Small Family Business/ Henceforward/Man of the Moment/The Revengers' Comedies (Parts One and Two)/ Wildest Dreams/Time of My Life/ Communicating Doors/Haunting Julia/By Jeeves/Things We Do for Love/ Comic Potential/House & Garden/Virtual Reality/ Damsels in Distress: GamePlan; FlatSpin; RôlePlay/Snake in the Grass/Sugar Daddies.

Alan Bleasdale (1946-	–	Are You Lonesome Tonight?/It's a Madhouse/Having a Ball/On the Ledge.
Christopher Hampton (1946-	–	When Did You Last See My Mother?/ Total Eclipse/The Philanthropist/Savages/ Treats/Les Liaisons Dangereuses/Tales from Hollywood.
(Sir) David Hare (1947-	–	The Secret Rapture/Racing Demon/ Murmuring Judges/The Absence of War/ Plenty/Knuckle/Fanshen/Teeth 'N' Smiles/ Pravda (with Howard Brenton)/Skylight/ Amy's View/The Judas Kiss/The Permanent Way.
Willy Russell (1948-	–	Educating Rita/Shirley Valentine/Blood Brothers/John, Paul, George, Ringo . . . and Bert/Stags and Hens (filmed as Dancin' Thru' the Dark)/Breezeblock Park/One for the Road/Our Day Out.
Terry Johnson (1955-	–	Insignificance/Hysteria/Dead Funny/Cleo, Camping, Emmanuelle and Dick/Unsuitable for Adults/Imagine Drowning/Hitchcock Blonde.
John Godber (1956-	–	Up 'N' Under/Bouncers/Teechers/Shakers/ September in the Rain/On the Piste/ Happy Families/Happy Jack/Salt of the Earth/April in Paris/The Office Party/ Lucky Sods/Gym and Tonic.
Jim Cartwright (1958-	–	Road/Bed/To (Two)/The Rise and Fall of Little Voice.
Patrick Marber (1964-	–	Dealer's Choice/Closer.

Scottish

(Sir) J(ames) M(atthew) Barrie (1860-1937)	–	Quality Street/The Admirable Crichton/ Peter Pan/What Every Woman Knows/ Dear Brutus/Mary Rose.
William Douglas-Home (1912-1992)	–	Now Barrabas/The Chiltern Hundreds/ The Manor of Northstead/The Secretary Bird/Lloyd George Knew My Father/ The Dame of Sark/The Kingfisher.

Irish

George Farquhar (1677-1707)	–	The Recruiting Officer/The Beaux' Stratagem/The Constant Couple.

Oliver Goldsmith (1728-1774)	– She Stoops to Conquer (subtitled – The Mistakes of a Night)/The Vicar of Wakefield (novel).
Dion Boucicault (*c.* 1820-1890)	– London Assurance/The Shaughraun/The Corsican Brothers/The Colleen Bawn.
Oscar Wilde (1854-1900)	– The Importance of Being Earnest/Lady Windermere's Fan/An Ideal Husband/A Woman of No Importance/Salome/The Picture of Dorian Gray (novel)/The Ballad of Reading Gaol (poem)/De profundis (prose).
George Bernard Shaw (1856-1950)	– Pygmalion (became My Fair Lady)/Saint Joan/Man and Superman/Arms and the Man/The Devil's Disciple/Major Barbara/ The Doctor's Dilemma/Caesar and Cleopatra/ The Millionairess/Heartbreak House/You Never Can Tell/Candida/Getting Married.
J(ohn) M(illington) Synge (1871-1909)	– The Playboy of the Western World.
Sean O'Casey (1884-1964)	– The Shadow of a Gunman/Juno and the Paycock/The Plough and the Stars/The Silver Tassie.
Samuel Beckett (1906-1989)	– Waiting for Godot/Endgame/Happy Days/ Krapp's Last Tape.
Brendan Behan (1923-1964)	– The Quare Fellow/The Hostage.
Brian Friel (1929-	– Dancing at Lughnasa/Philadelphia Here I Come!/Faith Healer/The Enemy Within/ The Freedom of the City/Translations/ Wonderful Tennessee/Molly Sweeney.

French

Pierre Corneille (1606-1684)	– Le Cid/Horace/Cinna/Polyeucte/Nicomède/ Le Menteur (The Liar).
Molière (1622-1673)	– Tartuffe/The Miser/The Misanthrope/The Imaginary Invalid/Le Bourgeois Gentil-homme/The School for Wives.
Jean Racine (1639-1699)	– Andromaque/Iphigénie/Phèdre/Britannicus/ Bajazet/Les Plaideurs/Bérénice/Esther/ Athalie.
Victor Hugo (1802-1885)	– Hernani/Le Roi s'amuse (basis for Verdi's Rigoletto)/Ruy Blas/Cromwell.

Georges Feydeau (1862-1921)	–	A Flea in Her Ear/An Absolute Turkey/ Pig in a Poke/Hotel Paradiso.
Edmond Rostand (1868-1918)	–	Cyrano de Bergerac.
Jean Cocteau (1889-1963)	–	Orpheus/Les Parents Terribles.
Jean Anouilh (1910-1987)	–	Antigone/L'Invitation au Château (Ring Round the Moon)/L'Alouette (The Lark)/ Becket/The Rehearsal/Waltz of the Toreadors/Eurydice.
Eugène Ionesco (1912-1994) (Romanian born)	–	The Bald Prima Donna/The Lesson/ The Chairs/Amédée/Rhinoceros.
Yasmina Reza (1959-	–	Art/The Unexpected Man/Life x 3.

German

Johann Wolfgang von Goethe (1749-1832)	–	Faust (Parts I and II)/Torquato Tasso.
Friedrich von Schiller (1759-1805)	–	Mary Stuart/William Tell/The Maid of Orleans/Wallenstein/Don Carlos/The Robbers.
Frank Wedekind (1864-1918)	–	Spring Awakening/Earth Spirit & Pandora's Box (the Lulu plays).
Bert(h)olt Brecht (1898-1956)	–	The Threepenny Opera/The Life of Galileo/The Resistible Rise of Arturo Ui/ The Good Woman of Setzuan/Mother Courage/The Caucasian Chalk Circle/ Fear and Misery in the Third Reich.

Italian

Luigi Pirandello (1867-1936)	–	Six Characters in Search of an Author/ Henry IV/The Rules of the Game/ Absolutely! (perhaps).
Eduardo de Filippo (1900-1984)	–	Filumena/Saturday, Sunday, Monday/La Grande Magia.

Spanish

Federico Garcia Lorca (1899-1936)	–	The House of Bernarda Alba/Yerma/ Blood Wedding.

Russian

Anton Chekhov (1860-1904)	–	The Seagull/Uncle Vanya/The Three Sisters/The Cherry Orchard/Ivanov/ Platonov/The Bear/The Proposal.

Norwegian

Henrik Ibsen (1828-1906)	–	Brand (lyrical)/Peer Gynt (lyrical)/Hedda Gabler/Ghosts/A Doll's House/The Master Builder/An Enemy of the People/The Wild Duck/Rosmersholm/John Gabriel Borkman.

Swedish

August Strindberg (1849-1912)	–	The Father/Miss Julie/The Creditors/The Dance of Death/A Dream Play.

American

Eugene O'Neill (1888-1953)	–	Mourning Becomes Electra/The Iceman Cometh/Long Day's Journey into Night/A Touch of the Poet.
Lillian Hellman (1905-1984)	–	The Children's Hour/The Little Foxes/Watch on the Rhine/Toys in the Attic.
Tennessee Williams (1914-1983)	–	The Glass Menagerie/A Streetcar Named Desire/Summer and Smoke/The Rose Tattoo/Cat on a Hot Tin Roof/The Night of the Iguana/Sweet Bird of Youth/Suddenly Last Summer/Small Craft Warnings.
Arthur Miller (1915-	–	Death of a Salesman/All My Sons/The Crucible/The Price/A View from the Bridge/The Man Who Had All the Luck/The American Clock/After the Fall/The Ride Down Mt. Morgan/The Last Yankee/Broken Glass.
Neil Simon (1927-	–	The Odd Couple/Barefoot in the Park/Come Blow Your Horn/Little Me/Sweet Charity/Plaza Suite/Promises, Promises/The Last of the Red Hot Lovers/The Gingerbread Lady (filmed as Only When I Laugh)/The Prisoner of Second Avenue/The Sunshine Boys/The Goodbye Girl/California Suite/Chapter Two/Seems Like Old Times/They're Playing Our Song/Brighton Beach Memoirs; Biloxi Blues; Broadway Bound (trilogy)/Rumors/Lost in Yonkers/The Good Doctor/Laughter on the 23rd Floor/The (Female) Odd Couple.

Edward Albee (1928-	–	Who's Afraid of Virginia Woolf?/The American Dream/Three Tall Women/A Delicate Balance.
John Guare (1938-	–	Six Degrees of Separation/The House of Blue Leaves.
Sam Shepard (1943-	–	The Tooth of Crime/Buried Child/True West/Fool for Love/Simpatico.
David Mamet (1947-	–	American Buffalo/Glengarry Glen Ross/ A Life in the Theatre/Speed-the-Plow/ Sexual Perversity in Chicago/Oleanna/The Cryptogram/Boston Marriage/Edmond.

Greek

Aeschylus (525-456 BC)	–	The Oresteia (Agamemnon; The Libation Bearers; The Eumenides)/Seven against Thebes/Prometheus Bound/The Persians/ The Suppliant Women.
Sophocles (496-406 BC)	–	Oedipus Tyrannus (Rex)/Oedipus at Colonus/ Antigone/Electra/Ajax/Philoctetes.
Euripides (*c.* 484-406/7 BC)	–	The Bacchae/Medea/Andromache/The Trojan Women/Electra/Iphigenia in Tauris/ Iphigenia at Aulis/Alcestis/Hippolytus/ Hecuba/Helen/ The Phoenician Women/Ion.
Aristophanes (*c.* 448-380 BC)	–	Lysistrata/The Clouds/The Birds/The Frogs/The Wasps/The Peace/Plutus/The Knights.

THE CINEMA

Film Directors

Director		*Well Known Films*
Robert Aldrich (1918-1983)	–	Apache/Vera Cruz/Kiss Me Deadly/The Big Knife/Attack!/Whatever Happened to Baby Jane?/Hush . . . Hush, Sweet Charlotte/The Flight of the Phoenix/The Dirty Dozen/The Killing of Sister George/The Choirboys.
Woody Allen (1935-	–	Take the Money and Run/Bananas/ Sleeper/Love and Death/Annie Hall/ Manhattan/Broadway Danny Rose/The Purple Rose of Cairo/Hannah and Her Sisters/Radio Days/Crimes and Misdemeanors/Alice/Husbands and Wives/ Shadows and Fog/Manhattan Murder Mystery/Bullets Over Broadway/Mighty Aphrodite/Everyone Says I Love You/ Deconstructing Harry/Celebrity/Small Time Crooks/Hollywood Ending/Curse of the Jade Scorpion.
Robert Altman (1925-	–	M*A*S*H/McCabe and Mrs Miller/ Nashville/A Wedding/Come Back to the Five and Dime, Jimmy Dean, Jimmy Dean/Fool for Love/The Player/Short Cuts/Kansas City/Gosford Park.
Lindsay Anderson (1923-1994)	–	This Sporting Life/If/O Lucky Man/ Britannia Hospital/The Whales of August.
Michael Anderson (1920-	–	The Dam Busters/Around the World in Eighty Days/Chase a Crooked Shadow/ Shake Hands with the Devil/The Wreck of the Mary Deare/The Naked Edge/ Operation Crossbow/The Quiller Memorandum/The Shoes of the Fisherman/ Conduct Unbecoming/Logan's Run/Orca.
Michelangelo Antonioni (1912-	–	Blow-Up/Zabriskie Point.

Michael Apted (1941-	–	Triple Echo/Stardust/Agatha/Coal Miner's Daughter/Gorky Park/Gorillas in the Mist/ 35 Up/Nell.
Anthony Asquith (1902-1968)	–	Pygmalion/French Without Tears/We Dive at Dawn/The Demi-Paradise/Fanny by Gaslight/The Way to the Stars/The Winslow Boy/The Browning Version/The Importance of Being Earnest/Orders to Kill/The Doctor's Dilemma/Libel/The Millionairess/ The V.I.P.s/ The Yellow Rolls-Royce.
(Lord) Richard Attenborough (1923-	–	Oh! What a Lovely War/Young Winston/ A Bridge Too Far/Magic/Gandhi/A Chorus Line/Cry Freedom/Chaplin/Shadowlands/In Love and War.
Robert Benton (1932-	–	Kramer vs. Kramer/Still of the Night/ Places in the Heart/Nobody's Fool.
Bruce Beresford (1940-	–	The Adventures of Barry McKenzie/The Getting of Wisdom/Breaker Morant/Tender Mercies/Crimes of the Heart/Driving Miss Daisy/Double Jeopardy.
Ingmar Bergman (1918-	–	The Seventh Seal/Wild Strawberries/ Smiles of a Summer Night/The Virgin Spring/Through a Glass Darkly/Scenes from a Marriage (TV)/Fanny and Alexander.
Bernardo Bertolucci (1940-	–	Last Tango in Paris/1900/The Last Emperor/The Sheltering Sky.
Peter Bogdanovich (1939-	–	Targets/The Last Picture Show/What's Up Doc?/Paper Moon/Daisy Miller/At Long Last Love/Nickelodeon/Mask/Noises Off.
John Boorman (1933-	–	Point Blank/Deliverance/The Emerald Forest/Hope and Glory/Beyond Rangoon/The Tailor of Panama.
John Boulting (1913-1985)	–	Brighton Rock/Lucky Jim/I'm All Right Jack/The Family Way/Twisted Nerve/ Endless Night.
Kenneth Branagh (1960-	–	Henry V (1989)/Dead Again/Peter's Friends/ Much Ado About Nothing/Mary Shelley's Frankenstein/In the Bleak Midwinter/ Hamlet (1996).

Mel Brooks (1926-	–	The Producers/The Twelve Chairs/Blazing Saddles/Young Frankenstein/Silent Movie/ High Anxiety/Spaceballs/Life Stinks/Robin Hood: Men in Tights/Dracula: Dead and Loving It.
Richard Brooks (1912-1992)	–	Blackboard Jungle/Elmer Gantry/In Cold Blood/Bite the Bullet.
Luis Buñuel (1900-1983)	–	Belle de Jour/The Discreet Charm of the Bourgeoisie/That Obscure Object of Desire.
Tim Burton (1960-	–	Beetlejuice/Batman/Edward Scissorhands/ Batman Returns/Ed Wood/Mars Attacks!/ Sleepy Hollow/Big Fish.
James Cameron (1954-	–	The Terminator/Aliens/The Abyss/ Terminator 2: Judgment Day/True Lies/ Titanic.
Jane Campion (1955-	–	An Angel at My Table/The Piano/The Portrait of a Lady/In the Cut.
Frank Capra (1897-1991)	–	It Happened One Night/Mr Deeds Goes to Town/Lost Horizon/You Can't Take It with You/Mr Smith Goes to Washington/Arsenic and Old Lace/It's a Wonderful Life.
John Carpenter (1948-	–	Dark Star/Assault on Precinct 13/ Halloween/The Fog/Escape from New York/ Christine/Starman.
Claude Chabrol (1930-	–	Les Biches/The Butcher/Violette Nozière.
Michael Cimino (1940-	–	The Deer Hunter/Heaven's Gate.
Chris Columbus (1959-	–	Home Alone (1 and 2)/Only the Lonely/Mrs Doubtfire/Nine Months/Stepmom/Harry Potter and the Philosopher's Stone/Harry Potter and the Chamber of Secrets.
Merian C. Cooper (1893-1973)	–	King Kong (co-director 1933 version).
Francis Ford Coppola (1939-	–	Finian's Rainbow/The Godfather (I, II and III)/Apocalypse Now/Bram Stoker's Dracula/The Conversation.

Roger Corman (1926-	–	Machine Gun Kelly/House of Usher/The Little Shop of Horrors (1960)/The Pit and the Pendulum/The Premature Burial/Tales of Terror/The Raven/The Masque of the Red Death/The Tomb of Ligeia/The St. Valentine's Day Massacre.
Constantin Costa-Gavras (1933-	–	The Sleeping Car Murder/Z/State of Siege/Missing/Betrayed/Music Box/Amen.
Charles Crichton (1910-1999)	–	The Lavender Hill Mob/The Titfield Thunderbolt/A Fish Called Wanda.
George Cukor (1899-1983)	–	Camille (1936)/The Women/The Philadelphia Story/Gaslight/Adam's Rib/Edward My Son/BornYesterday/Pat and Mike/A Star Is Born (1954)/Wild Is the Wind/My Fair Lady/Travels with My Aunt/Rich and Famous.
Michael Curtiz (1888-1962)	–	Angels with Dirty Faces/The Sea Hawk/Yankee Doodle Dandy/Casablanca/Mildred Pierce/Night and Day/White Christmas.
Stephen Daldry (1961-	–	Billy Elliot/The Hours.
Jules Dassin (1911-	–	The Naked City/Rififi/Never on Sunday/Topkapi/Circle of Two.
Cecil B(lount) DeMille (1881-1959)	–	King of Kings (1927)/The Plainsman (1936)/Samson and Delilah (1949)/The Greatest Show on Earth/The Ten Commandments (2 versions 1923 and 1956).
Brian de Palma (1940-	–	Carrie/Dressed to Kill/Body Double/The Untouchables/Carlito's Way.
Vittorio de Sica (1901-1974)	–	Bicycle Thieves/Miracle in Milan/Two Women/Yesterday, Today and Tomorrow/Marriage Italian Style/After The Fox/Woman Times Seven/The Garden of the Finzi-Continis.
Jonathan Demme (1944-	–	Last Embrace/Melvin and Howard/Married to the Mob/The Silence of the Lambs/Philadelphia.
Edward Dmytryk (1908-1999)	–	Crossfire/The Caine Mutiny/Raintree County/The Young Lions/Walk on the Wild Side/The Carpetbaggers/Mirage/Anzio/Shalako.

Stanley Donen (1924-	–	On the Town/Singin' in the Rain/Seven Brides for Seven Brothers/Deep in My Heart/It's Always Fair Weather/Funny Face/ The Pajama Game/DamnYankees/Charade/ Arabesque/Two for the Road/Bedazzled/ Staircase/The Little Prince/Movie Movie/ Blame It on Rio.
Richard Donner (1939-	–	The Omen/Superman/Lethal Weapon (1, 2, 3 and 4)/Maverick.
Clint Eastwood (1930-	–	Play Misty for Me/The Outlaw Josey Wales/ The Gauntlet/Unforgiven/A Perfect World/ The Bridges of Madison County/Mystic River.
Blake Edwards (1922-	–	Breakfast at Tiffany's/Days of Wine and Roses/The Pink Panther series (including A Shot in the Dark)/The Great Race/The Tamarind Seed/Micki and Maude.
Sergei Eisenstein (1898-1948)	–	Strike/The Battleship Potemkin/October/ Alexander Nevsky/Ivan the Terrible (Parts 1 and 2).
Nora Ephron (1941-	–	Sleepless in Seattle/Michael/You've Got Mail.
(Sir) Richard Eyre (1943-	–	The Ploughman's Lunch/Iris.
Federico Fellini (1920-1993)	–	La Strada/La Dolce Vita/8½/Juliet of the Spirits/Satyricon/Ginger and Fred.
Victor Fleming (1883-1949)	–	The Virginian (1929)/The Wizard of Oz/Gone with the Wind/Dr Jekyll and Mr Hyde (1941).
Bryan Forbes (1926-	–	Whistle Down the Wind/The L-Shaped Room/Séance on a Wet Afternoon/King Rat/ The Wrong Box/The Whisperers/The Stepford Wives/International Velvet.
John Ford (1895-1973)	–	Stagecoach/Young Mr Lincoln/The Grapes of Wrath/How Green Was My Valley/Rio Grande/The Quiet Man/Mister Roberts (co-director)/Cheyenne Autumn.
Milos Forman (1932-	–	One Flew Over the Cuckoo's Nest/Hair/ Ragtime/Amadeus.
Bill Forsyth (1947-	–	Gregory's Girl/Local Hero/Comfort and Joy.
Bob Fosse (1927-1987)	–	Sweet Charity/Cabaret/Lenny/All That Jazz/Star 80.

John Frankenheimer (1930-2002)	–	The Manchurian Candidate/Birdman of Alcatraz/Seven Days in May.
Lewis Gilbert (1920-	–	Reach for the Sky/The Admirable Crichton/ Carve Her Name with Pride/Sink the Bismarck/Alfie/You Only Live Twice/The Spy Who Loved Me/Moonraker/Educating Rita/ Not Quite Jerusalem/Stepping Out.
Sidney Gilliat (1908-1994)	–	The Story of Gilbert and Sullivan/The Constant Husband/Only Two Can Play/ Endless Night.
Jean-Luc Godard (1930-	–	À Bout de Souffle (Breathless) (1960).
Peter Greenaway (1942-	–	The Draughtsman's Contract/Drowning by Numbers/The Cook, the Thief, His Wife and Her Lover/Prospero's Books/ The Baby of Macon.
D(avid) W(ark) Griffith (1875-1948)	–	The Birth of a Nation/Intolerance.
Lasse Hallström (1946-	–	Abba – the Movie/My Life as a Dog/What's Eating Gilbert Grape?/The Cider House Rules/Chocolat/The Shipping News.
Henry Hathaway (1898-1985)	–	The Lives of a Bengal Lancer/The House on 92nd Street/Kiss of Death/Call Northside 777/Fourteen Hours/Niagara/23 Paces to Baker Street/North to Alaska/The Sons of Katie Elder/Nevada Smith/True Grit.
Howard Hawks (1896-1977)	–	Scarface (1932)/Bringing Up Baby/His Girl Friday/Ball of Fire/To Have and Have Not/The Big Sleep/Red River/Gentlemen Prefer Blondes/Rio Bravo.
George Roy Hill (1922-2002)	–	Period of Adjustment/Butch Cassidy and the Sundance Kid/The Sting.
Arthur Hiller (1923-	–	The Americanization of Emily/The Out-of-Towners/Love Story/Plaza Suite/The Hospital/W.C.Fields and Me/Silver Streak/ The In-Laws/Author! Author!/Romantic Comedy/Outrageous Fortune.

(Sir) Alfred Hitchcock (1899-1980)	–	Blackmail/The Thirty-Nine Steps (1935)/ The Lady Vanishes (1938)/Jamaica Inn/ Rebecca/Suspicion/Saboteur/Shadow of a Doubt/Lifeboat/Spellbound/Notorious/Rope/ Stage Fright/Strangers on a Train/I Confess/Dial M for Murder/Rear Window/ To Catch a Thief/The Man Who Knew Too Much/The Wrong Man/Vertigo/North by Northwest/Psycho/The Birds/Marnie/Torn Curtain/Frenzy/Family Plot.
Ron Howard (1953-	–	Splash!/Cocoon/Willow/Parenthood/Back-draft/Far and Away/Apollo 13/Ransom/A Beautiful Mind.
Hugh Hudson (1936-	–	Chariots of Fire/Greystoke/Revolution (1985).
Howard Hughes (1905-1976)	–	Hell's Angels/The Outlaw (with Howard Hawks).
John Huston (1906-1987)	–	The Maltese Falcon/Treasure of the Sierra Madre/Key Largo/The Asphalt Jungle/The Red Badge of Courage/The African Queen/ Moulin Rouge/Moby Dick/Heaven Knows Mr Allison/The Misfits/Freud/The List of Adrian Messenger/The Night of the Iguana/ Annie/Prizzi's Honor/The Dead.
James Ivory (1928-	–	Shakespeare Wallah/The Europeans/Heat and Dust/The Bostonians/A Room with a View/Maurice/Howard's End/The Remains of the Day/Jefferson in Paris/Surviving Picasso/The Golden Bowl.
Peter Jackson (1961-	–	Heavenly Creatures/The Frighteners/The Lord of the Rings – The Fellowship of the Ring/The Two Towers/The Return of the King.
Derek Jarman (1942-1994)	–	Sebastiane/Caravaggio/Edward II/Blue.
Norman Jewison (1926-	–	Forty Pounds of Trouble/The Thrill of It All/ Send Me No Flowers/The Cincinnati Kid/In the Heat of the Night/The Thomas Crown Affair/Fiddler on the Roof/Jesus Christ Superstar/Rollerball/And Justice for All/ Best Friends/A Soldier's Story/Agnes of God/ Moonstruck/Only You.

Roland Joffé (1945-	–	The Killing Fields/The Mission/City of Joy/ The Scarlet Letter.
Neil Jordan (1950-	–	The Company of Wolves/Mona Lisa/The Crying Game/Interview with the Vampire/ Michael Collins/The End of the Affair.
Elia Kazan (1909-2003)	–	A Tree Grows in Brooklyn/Gentleman's Agreement/A Streetcar Named Desire/Viva Zapata/On the Waterfront/East of Eden/ Baby Doll/A Face in the Crowd/Splendor in the Grass/The Last Tycoon.
(Sir) Alexander Korda (1893-1956)	–	The Private Life of Henry VIII/ Rembrandt.
Stanley Kramer (1913-2001)	–	Not as a Stranger/The Pride and the Passion/The Defiant Ones/On the Beach/ Inherit the Wind/Judgment at Nuremberg/ It's a Mad Mad Mad Mad World/Ship of Fools/Guess Who's Coming to Dinner.
Stanley Kubrick (1928-1999)	–	The Killing/Paths of Glory/Spartacus/ Lolita/Dr Strangelove/2001: A Space Odyssey/A Clockwork Orange/The Shining/ Full Metal Jacket/Eyes Wide Shut.
Fritz Lang (1890-1976)	–	Metropolis/Fury/You Only Live Once/Man Hunt/The Woman in the Window/Clash by Night/The Blue Gardenia/The Big Heat/ While the City Sleeps/Beyond a Reasonable Doubt.
Frank Launder (1907-1997)	–	The Blue Lagoon/The Happiest Days of Your Life/The Belles of St. Trinian's/ Geordie/The Bridal Path.
(Sir) David Lean (1908-1991)	–	In Which We Serve (co-director with Noël Coward)/This Happy Breed/Blithe Spirit/ Brief Encounter/Great Expectations/Oliver Twist/Hobson's Choice/The Bridge on the River Kwai/Lawrence of Arabia/Dr Zhivago/ Ryan's Daughter/A Passage to India.
Ang Lee (1954-	–	The Wedding Banquet/Eat Drink Man Woman/Sense and Sensibility/Crouching Tiger, Hidden Dragon.
Mike Leigh (1943-	–	Abigail's Party (TV)/Nuts in May (TV)/High Hopes/Life Is Sweet/Secrets and Lies/Topsy-Turvy.
Claude Lelouch (1937-	–	Un Homme et Une Femme (A Man and a Woman)/Vivre Pour Vivre (Live for Life).

Barry Levinson (1942-	–	Diner/The Natural/Young Sherlock Holmes/Tin Men/Good Morning, Vietnam/Rain Man/Avalon/Bugsy/Toys/Disclosure/Sleepers/Wag the Dog.
Joshua Logan (1908-1988)	–	Picnic/Bus Stop/South Pacific/Camelot/Paint Your Wagon.
Joseph Losey (1909-1984)	–	The Servant/King and Country/Accident/The Go-Between/The Romantic Englishwoman/Steaming.
Ernst Lubitsch (1892-1947)	–	Trouble in Paradise/Ninotchka/The Shop Around the Corner/To Be or Not to Be (1942)/Heaven Can Wait (1943).
George Lucas (1944-	–	American Graffiti/Star Wars/Star Wars Episode I: The Phantom Menace/Episode II: Attack of the Clones.
Baz Luhrmann (1962-	–	Strictly Ballroom/Romeo and Juliet (1996)/Moulin Rouge.
Sidney Lumet (1924-	–	Twelve Angry Men/A View from the Bridge/Long Day's Journey into Night/Fail-Safe/The Pawnbroker/The Hill/The Group/The Offence/Serpico/Murder on the Orient Express/Dog Day Afternoon/Network/Equus/The Wiz/Deathtrap/The Verdict/Daniel/The Morning After/Family Business.
Alexander MacKendrick (1912-1993)	–	Whisky Galore/The Man in the White Suit/Mandy/The Ladykillers/Sweet Smell of Success/Sammy Going South/A High Wind in Jamaica.
John Madden (1949-	–	Mrs Brown/Shakespeare in Love/Captain Corelli's Mandolin.
Louis Malle (1932-1995)	–	Zazie dans le Métro/Lacombe Lucien/Atlantic City/Au Revoir, les Enfants.
Joseph L(eo) Mankiewicz (1909-1993)	–	A Letter to Three Wives/House of Strangers/No Way Out (1950)/All About Eve/Julius Caesar/The Barefoot Contessa/Guys and Dolls/The Quiet American/Suddenly Last Summer/Cleopatra/Sleuth.
Anthony Mann (1906-1967)	–	Winchester '73/The Tall Target/Bend of the River/The Glenn Miller Story/The Man from Laramie/El Cid/The Fall of the Roman Empire/The Heroes of Telemark.
Rob Marshall (1960-	–	Chicago.

Sam Mendes (1965-	–	American Beauty/Road to Perdition.
Lewis Milestone (1895-1980)	–	All Quiet on the Western Front/Of Mice and Men/Les Misérables (1952).
Anthony Minghella (1954-	–	Truly Madly Deeply/Mr Wonderful/The English Patient/The Talented Mr Ripley/ Cold Mountain.
Vincente Minnelli (1903-1986)	–	Cabin in the Sky/Ziegfeld Follies/Meet Me in St. Louis/The Clock/The Pirate/ Madame Bovary/Father of the Bride (1950)/An American in Paris/The Band Wagon/Brigadoon/Kismet/Lust for Life/ Tea and Sympathy/Gigi/Some Came Running/Bells Are Ringing/The Sandpiper/ On a Clear Day You Can See Forever.
Mike Newell (1942-	–	Dance with a Stranger/Enchanted April/ Four Weddings and a Funeral/An Awfully Big Adventure/Donnie Brasco.
Mike Nichols (1931-	–	Who's Afraid of Virginia Woolf?/The Graduate/Catch 22/Carnal Knowledge/ Silkwood/Heartburn/Biloxi Blues/Working Girl/Postcards from the Edge/The Birdcage/Primary Colors.
Alan J(ay) Pakula (1928-1998)	–	Klute/All the President's Men/Starting Over/Sophie's Choice/Presumed Innocent/ The Pelican Brief.
Alan Parker (1944-	–	Bugsy Malone/Midnight Express/Fame/ Birdy/Mississippi Burning/The Commitments/Evita/Angela's Ashes.
Pier Paolo Pasolini (1922-1975)	–	The Gospel According to St. Matthew/ Theorem/Decameron/The Canterbury Tales/ The Arabian Nights.
Sam Peckinpah (1925-1984)	–	The Wild Bunch/Straw Dogs/Junior Bonner/ The Getaway/Pat Garrett and Billy the Kid.
Arthur Penn (1922-	–	The Miracle Worker/Bonnie and Clyde/Alice's Restaurant/Little Big Man/Night Moves.
Roman Polanski (1933-	–	Knife in the Water/Repulsion/Rosemary's Baby/Chinatown/Tess/Bitter Moon/Death and the Maiden/The Pianist.
Sydney Pollack (1934-	–	The Slender Thread/They Shoot Horses, Don't They?/The Way We Were/Three Days of the Condor/Absence of Malice/Tootsie/Out of Africa/The Firm.

Michael Powell (1905-1990) Emeric Pressburger (1902-1988)	–	One of Our Aircraft is Missing/The Life and Death of Colonel Blimp/I Know Where I'm Going/A Matter of Life and Death (Stairway to Heaven)/Black Narcissus/The Red Shoes/The Small Back Room/The Battle of the River Plate (Pursuit of the Graf Spee)/Ill Met by Moonlight (Night Ambush).
Otto Preminger (1906-1986)	–	Laura/Forever Amber/River of No Return/ Carmen Jones/The Man with the Golden Arm/Porgy and Bess/Anatomy of a Murder/ Exodus/Advise and Consent/Tell Me That You Love Me, Junie Moon.
Nicholas Ray (1911-1979)	–	They Live by Night/Rebel Without a Cause/ Bigger Than Life/King of Kings (1961)/55 Days at Peking.
Robert Redford (1937-	–	Ordinary People/A River Runs Through It/ Quiz Show/The Horse Whisperer.
(Sir) Carol Reed (1906-1976)	–	The Stars Look Down/Night Train to Munich/Kipps/The Young Mr Pitt/The Way Ahead/Odd Man Out/The Fallen Idol/The Third Man/Outcast of the Islands/A Kid for Two Farthings/Trapeze/Our Man in Havana/ The Running Man (1963)/The Agony and the Ecstasy/Oliver!
Jean Renoir (1894-1979)	–	La Grande Illusion/La Bête Humaine/ La Règle du Jeu/The Southerner.
Tony Richardson (1928-1991)	–	Look Back in Anger/The Entertainer/A Taste of Honey/The Loneliness of the Long Distance Runner/Tom Jones/The Loved One/ The Charge of the Light Brigade/Ned Kelly.
Leni Riefenstahl (1902-2003)	–	Triumph of the Will (the Nuremberg Rally)/ The Olympic Games (1936).
Martin Ritt (1920-1990)	–	The Long Hot Summer/The Black Orchid/ Hud/The Outrage/The Spy Who Came in from the Cold/Hombre/The Brotherhood/The Molly Maguires/The Great White Hope/Pete 'n Tillie/ The Front/Norma Rae/Cross Creek/Stanley & Iris.
Nicolas Roeg (1928-	–	Performance (co-director)/Don't Look Now/ The Man Who Fell to Earth/Bad Timing/ Insignificance/Castaway/The Witches.

Herbert Ross (1927-2001)	–	Goodbye Mr Chips (1969)/The Owl and the Pussycat/Play It Again Sam/Funny Lady/ The Sunshine Boys/The Seven Percent Solution/The Turning Point/The Goodbye Girl/Pennies from Heaven (1981)/Footloose/ Steel Magnolias/My Blue Heaven.
Roberto Rossellini (1906-1977)	–	Rome, Open City/Germany, Year Zero.
Ken Russell (1927-	–	Women in Love/The Music Lovers/The Devils/The Boy Friend/Savage Messiah/ Mahler/Tommy/Lisztomania/Valentino/ The Rainbow.
Fred Schepisi (1939-	–	Plenty/Roxanne/A Cry in the Dark/The Russia House/I.Q./Six Degrees of Separation.
John Schlesinger (1926-2003)	–	A Kind of Loving/Billy Liar/Darling/Far from the Madding Crowd/Midnight Cowboy/ Sunday, Bloody Sunday/Marathon Man/ Yanks/Pacific Heights/Eye for an Eye.
Martin Scorsese (1942-	–	Mean Streets/Alice Doesn't Live Here Anymore/Taxi Driver/New York, New York/ The Last Waltz/Raging Bull/King of Comedy/The Color of Money/GoodFellas/ Cape Fear/The Age of Innocence/Gangs of New York.
(Sir) Ridley Scott (1939-	–	The Duellists/Alien/Blade Runner/Someone to Watch Over Me/Thelma and Louise/1492: Conquest of Paradise/White Squall/G.I. Jane/Gladiator/Hannibal/Black Hawk Down.
Jim Sheridan (1949-	–	My Left Foot/In the Name of the Father/In America.
Steven Soderbergh (1963-	–	sex, lies and videotape/Kafka/King of the Hill/Out of Sight/The Limey/Erin Brockovich/ Traffic/Ocean's Eleven (2002)/Solaris.
Steven Spielberg (1946-	–	Jaws/1941/Close Encounters of the Third Kind/Raiders of the Lost Ark/E.T./Indiana Jones and the Temple of Doom/The Color Purple/Empire of the Sun/Always/Hook/ Jurassic Park/Schindler's List/The Lost World: Jurassic Park/Saving Private Ryan/ AI/Minority Report/Catch Me If You Can.

George Stevens (1904-1975)	–	Gunga Din/Penny Serenade/Woman of the Year/I Remember Mama/A Place in the Sun/Shane/Giant/The Diary of Anne Frank/ The Greatest Story Ever Told.
Oliver Stone (1946-	–	Platoon/Wall Street/Born on the Fourth of July/JFK/Heaven and Earth/Nixon.
John Sturges (1911-1992)	–	Bad Day at Black Rock/Gunfight at the O.K. Corral/The Magnificent Seven/The Great Escape/Ice Station Zebra/The Eagle Has Landed.
Quentin Tarantino (1963-	–	Reservoir Dogs/Pulp Fiction.
Jacques Tati (1908-1982)	–	Jour de Fête/Monsieur Hulot's Holiday/Mon Oncle/Playtime/Traffic.
François Truffaut (1932-1984)	–	The Four Hundred Blows (Les Quatre Cents Coups)/Shoot the Piano Player/Jules and Jim/ Fahrenheit 451/The Bride Wore Black/ Stolen Kisses/The Last Métro.
Charles Vidor (1900-1959)	–	Blind Alley/My Son, My Son/Ladies in Retirement/Cover Girl/A Song to Remember/Gilda/Hans Christian Andersen/ Love Me or Leave Me/The Joker Is Wild (All the Way)/A Farewell to Arms.
King Vidor (1894-1982)	–	The Champ (1931)/Our Daily Bread/Stella Dallas/The Citadel/Northwest Passage/H.M. Pulham Esq./Duel in the Sun/The Fountainhead/War and Peace/Solomon and Sheba.
Luchino Visconti (1906-1976)	–	White Nights (1957)/Rocco and His Brothers/The Leopard/The Damned/Death in Venice.
Peter Weir (1944-	–	Picnic at Hanging Rock/The Last Wave/ Gallipoli/The Year of Living Dangerously/ Witness/The Mosquito Coast/Dead Poets Society/Green Card/The Truman Show/ Master and Commander: The Far Side of the World.
Orson Welles (1915-1985)	–	Citizen Kane/The Magnificent Ambersons/ The Stranger/The Lady from Shanghai/ Macbeth/Othello/Touch of Evil/The Trial/ Chimes at Midnight/The Immortal Story/ F. for Fake.

William Wellman (1896-1975) – Wings/Public Enemy/Nothing Sacred/A Star Is Born/Beau Geste/The Light that Failed/The Ox-Bow Incident/Roxie Hart/The Story of G.I. Joe/The Iron Curtain/The Next Voice You Hear/Across the Wide Missouri/The High and the Mighty.

Wim Wenders (1945- – The Goalkeeper's Fear of the Penalty Kick/Kings of the Road/The American Friend/Hammett/Paris, Texas/Wings of Desire/Faraway, So Close!

James Whale (1896-1957) – Frankenstein/The Old Dark House (1932)/The Invisible Man/Bride of Frankenstein/Showboat (1936)/The Man in the Iron Mask (1939).

Billy Wilder (1906-2002) – Double Indemnity/The Lost Weekend/A Foreign Affair/Sunset Boulevard/Ace in the Hole/Stalag 17/The Seven Year Itch/The Spirit of St. Louis/Love in the Afternoon/Witness for the Prosecution/Some Like It Hot/The Apartment/One Two Three/Irma La Douce/The Fortune Cookie/The Private Life of Sherlock Holmes/Avanti/The Front Page/Buddy Buddy.

Michael Winner (1935- – The Jokers/Hannibal Brooks/Death Wish (I, II and III)/Appointment with Death/A Chorus of Disapproval.

Robert Wise (1914- – The Body Snatcher/The Set-Up/The Day the Earth Stood Still/Somebody Up There Likes Me/I Want to Live/West Side Story/The Sound of Music/The Sand Pebbles/Star!/The Andromeda Strain/Audrey Rose/Star Trek.

WilliamWyler (1902-1981) – Jezebel/Wuthering Heights (1939)/The Letter/The Westerner/The Little Foxes/Mrs Miniver/The Best Years of Our Lives/The Heiress/Detective Story/Roman Holiday/The Desperate Hours (1955)/Friendly Persuasion/The Big Country/Ben Hur/The Children's Hour/The Collector/How to Steal a Million/Funny Girl/The Liberation of L.B. Jones.

Peter Yates (1929-	–	Robbery/Bullitt/Murphy's War/The Hot Rock/The Friends of Eddie Coyle/For Pete's Sake/Breaking Away/The Dresser/Suspect/ The House on Carroll Street.
Franco Zeffirelli (1922-	–	The Taming of the Shrew/Romeo and Juliet/ Brother Sun and Sister Moon/Jesus of Nazareth (TV)/The Champ (1979)/Endless Love/La Traviata/Otello/Hamlet (1990)/ Jane Eyre (1996)/Tea with Mussolini.
Robert Zemeckis (1952-	–	Romancing the Stone/Back to the Future (Parts I, II and III)/Who Framed Roger Rabbit?/Death Becomes Her/Forrest Gump.
Fred Zinnemann (1907-1997)	–	The Seventh Cross/Act of Violence/The Men (Battle Stripe)/High Noon/The Member of the Wedding/From Here to Eternity/ Oklahoma!/A Hatful of Rain/The Nun's Story/The Sundowners/A Man for All Seasons/The Day of the Jackal/Julia.

ANIMAL WORLD

Some Facts about Dogs

Old English Mastiff St. Bernard	–	heaviest breeds.
Great Dane Irish Wolf Hound	–	tallest breeds.
Yorkshire Terrier Toy Poodle Chihuahua	–	smallest breeds.
Chihuahua	–	named after largest state of Mexico.
Basenji	–	African hunting dog with (virtually) no bark.
Chow (-chow)	–	Chinese breed of dog which has a black tongue.
Pekingese (Pekinese)	–	dwarf pug-dog originally from Peking.
Dachshund	–	derives its name from German for 'badger-dog'.
Spaniel	–	derives its name from old French word meaning 'Spanish'.
Terrier	–	derives its name from 'terra' meaning 'land' or 'earth' because it would follow burrowing animals underground.
Corgi	–	Welsh breed of dog whose name means 'dwarf' – traditionally kept as a Royal pet since 1933.
Lurcher	–	properly, cross between a greyhound and a collie (variety of sheepdog).
Whippet	–	cross between a greyhound and a spaniel or terrier.

Dwelling Places of Creatures

Creature		*Dwelling Place*	*Creature*		*Dwelling Place*
Ape	–	tree-nest.	Lion	–	den, lair.
Badger	–	set(t), earth.	Mole	–	fortress.
Bear	–	den, lair.	Mouse	–	hole, nest.
Beaver	–	lodge.	Otter	–	holt.
Bee	–	hive.	Rabbit	–	burrow, warren.
Bird	–	nest.	Spider	–	web.
Eagle	–	eyrie.	Squirrel	–	drey.
Fox	–	earth, lair.	Tiger	–	lair.
Hare	–	form.	Wasp	–	nest, vespiary.

A fox's tail is called a **brush**.
An otter's tail is called a **pole**.
A rabbit's tail is called a **scut**.

Group Names – Collective Nouns of Animals

Antelopes	–	Herd/Troop.
Apes	–	Shrewdness.
Asses	–	Pace/Herd.
Baboons	–	Troop.
Badgers	–	Cete.
Bears	–	Sleuth.
Beavers	–	Colony.
Boars	–	Sounder.
Buffaloes	–	Herd.
Cats	–	Clowder/Clutter.
Cattle	–	Herd/Drove.
Colts	–	Rag.
Cows	–	Herd.
Curs	–	Cowardice.
Deer	–	Herd.
Dogs	–	Pack.
Elephants	–	Herd.
Elk	–	Gang.
Foxes	–	Skulk.
Frogs	–	Army.
Giraffes	–	Herd.
Goats	–	Tribe/Flock/Herd.
Hares	–	Down/Husk.
Hedgehogs	–	Array.
Hogs	–	Sounder.
Horses	–	Haras/Stable/Stud.
Hounds	–	Pack/Cry/Mute.
Kangaroos	–	Mob/Troop.
Kittens	–	Kindle.
Leopards	–	Leap.
Lions	–	Pride/Troop.
Mares	–	Stud.
Martens	–	Richesse.
Moles	–	Labour.
Monkeys	–	Troop.
Mules	–	Barren.
Oxen (wild)	–	Drove/Herd.
(domestic)	–	Team/Yoke.
Pigs/Pups/Cubs	–	Litter.
Ponies	–	Herd.
Rabbits	–	Nest.
Racehorses	–	String/Field.
Rhinoceroses	–	Crash.
Roe deer	–	Bevy.
Sheep	–	Flock.
Snakes	–	Den/Pit.
Swine	–	Herd.
Tigers	–	Ambush.
Vipers	–	Nest.
Wolves	–	Pack/Rout.
Zebras	–	Herd.

Marine and Aquatic Mammals

Dolphins	–	School.
Otters	–	Family.
Porpoises	–	School/Gam.
Seals	–	Herd/Pod.
Whales	–	School/Pod (when travelling).

Fish

Fish	–	Shoal/Catch/Draught/Haul.
Herring(s)	–	Shoal/Glean.
Trout	–	Hover.
Whiting	–	Pod.

Birds

Birds – Congregation/Flight/Flock/Volery/Volley

Bitterns – Sedge/Siege.
Capercaillie – Tok.
Chickens/Hens – Brood.
Choughs – Chattering.
Coots – Covert.
Cranes – Herd/Sedge/Siege.
Crows – Murder.
Curlews – Herd.
Doves – Dole/Flight.
Ducks – Paddling (on water) Team (in flight).
Eagles – Convocation.
Geese – Flock/Gaggle/ Skein (in flight).
(Gold)finches – Charm.
Grouse – Brood/Covey/Pack.
Gulls – Colony.
Hawks/Falcons – Cast.
Herons – Sedge/Siege.
Lapwings – Desert.
Larks – Exaltation.
Magpies – Tiding/Tittering.
Nightingales – Watch.
Owls – Parliament.
Partridges – Covey.
Peacocks – Muster.
Penguins – Colony/Rookery.
Pheasants – Nide/Nye.
Pigeons – Flight/Flock.
Plovers – Stand/Wing.
Poultry (domestic) – Run.
Quails – Bevy.
Ravens – Unkindness.
Rooks – Building/Clamour.
Ruffs – Herd/Hill.
Sandpipers – Fling.
Snipe – Wisp/Walk.
Sparrows – Host.
Starlings – Chattering/ Murmuration.
Storks – Mustering.
Swallows – Flight/Gulp.
Swans – Bevy/Herd.
Swifts – Flock.
Thrushes – Mutation.
Turkeys – Rafter.
Widgeon – Bunch/Company/Coil. Knob (on water)/ Flight (in the air).
Wildfowl – Plump/Sord/Sute.
Woodcocks – Fall.
Woodpeckers – Descent.
Wrens – Herd.

Insects

Ants – Army/Column/Swarm.
Bees – Swarm/Hive.
Caterpillars – Army.
Flies – Swarm.
Gnats – Cloud/Swarm.
Insects – Swarm.
Locusts – Cloud/Horde/Plague/Swarm.
Wasps – Nest.

Creatures and their Young

Creature	*Male*	*Female*	*Young*
Antelope	Buck	Doe	Kid/Fawn.
Badger	Boar	Sow	Cub.
Bear	Boar	Sow/She-bear	Cub.
Beaver			Kit.
Butterfly/Moth			Caterpillar (grub).
Cat	Tom	Queen	Kitten.
Deer (Fallow)	Buck	Doe	Fawn.
Dog	Dog	Bitch	Puppy.
Donkey/Ass	Jack	Jenny	Foal.
Duck	Drake	Duck	Duckling.
Eagle			Eaglet.
Eel			Elver.
Elephant	Bull	Cow	Calf.
Ferret	Hob	Gill/Jill	Kitten.
Fowl (domestic)	Cock/Rooster	Hen	Chick(en).
Fox	Dog-fox	Vixen	Cub.
Frog			Tadpole (larva).
Giraffe	Bull	Cow	Calf.
Goat	Billy-goat	Nanny(-goat)	Kid.
Goose	Gander	Goose	Gosling.
Hare	Buck	Doe	Leveret.
Hedgehog	Boar	Sow	Urchin/Hoglet.
Hippopotamus	Bull	Cow	Calf.
Horse	Stallion/Colt	Mare/Filly	Foal.
Kangaroo	Boomer/Buck	Doe	Joey.
Lion	Lion	Lioness	Cub.
Ostrich	Cock	Hen	Chick.
Owl			Owlet.
Ox (Cattle)	Bull	Cow	Calf.
Pig	Boar	Sow	Piglet.
Pigeon/Rook			Squab.
Rabbit	Buck	Doe	Kit(ten).
Red deer	Hart/Stag	Hind/Roe	Fawn.
Rhinoceros	Bull	Cow	Calf.
Salmon	Cock		Grilse/Parr/Smolt.
Seal			Pup.
Sheep	Ram/Tup	Ewe	Lamb.
Swan	Cob	Pen	Cygnet.

Tiger	Tiger	Tigress	Cub.
Whale	Bull	Cow	Calf.
Wolf	Wolf	She-wolf	Cub.
Zebra	Stallion	Mare	Foal.

Animal Adjectives

Anguine	–	of or like a snake.
Anserine	–	pertaining to geese.
Apian	–	pertaining to bees.
Aquiline	–	of or like an eagle; curved.
Asinine	–	pertaining to asses; stupid.
Avian	–	pertaining to birds.
Bovine	–	pertaining to cattle; ox-like.
Canine	–	of or like a dog; a type of tooth.
Caprine	–	of or like a goat; (hence, capricious).
Cervine	–	of or like a deer.
Columbine	–	of or like a dove.
Corvine	–	of or like a crow.
Elephantine	–	of elephants; huge, clumsy, unwieldy.
Equine	–	of or like a horse.
Feline	–	of cats; catlike.
Formic	–	pertaining to ants.
Hircine	–	goatlike.
Leonine	–	of or like a lion.
Leporine	–	of or like hares.
Lupine	–	of or like a wolf.
Murine	–	of or like mice.
Ovine	–	of or like sheep.
Passerine	–	of or like a sparrow, sparrow-like.
Pavonine	–	of or like a peacock.
Piscine	–	of fish.
Porcine	–	of or like pigs.
Psittacine	–	of or like a parrot.
Simian	–	of an ape, apelike, monkey-like.
Tigrine	–	of or like a tiger.
Turdine	–	of or like a thrush.
Ursine	–	of or like a bear.
Vaccine	–	of or derived from a cow.
Vulpine	–	of or like a fox; crafty, cunning.

WORDS

Phobias

Claustrophobia	–	Fear of confined spaces.
Agoraphobia	–	Fear of open spaces.
Ochlophobia	–	Fear of crowds.
Acrophobia	–	Fear of heights.
Hydrophobia	–	Fear of water.
Pyrophobia	–	Fear of fire.
Brontophobia	–	Fear of thunder.
Astraphobia	–	Fear of lightning.
Ombrophobia	–	Fear of rain.
Nyctophobia	–	Fear of darkness.
Sciophobia	–	Fear of shadows.
Bibliophobia	–	Fear of books.
Erg(asi)ophobia	–	Fear of work.
Xenophobia	–	Fear of foreigners.
Triskaidekaphobia	–	Fear of number 13.
Zoophobia	–	Fear of animals.
Arachnophobia	–	Fear of spiders.
Apiphobia	–	Fear of bees.
Musophobia	–	Fear of mice.
Ail(o)urophobia	–	Fear of cats.
Cynophobia	–	Fear of dogs.
Hippophobia	–	Fear of horses.
Oph(id)iophobia	–	Fear of snakes.
Ornithophobia	–	Fear of birds.
Dendrophobia	–	Fear of trees.
Androphobia	–	Fear of men.
Gynophobia	–	Fear of women.
Gam(et)ophobia	–	Fear of marriage.
Gymnophobia	–	Fear of nudity.
Lalophobia	–	Fear of speech.
Phonophobia	–	Fear of noise/speaking aloud.
Haematophobia	–	Fear of blood.
Algophobia	–	Fear of pain.
Nosophobia	–	Fear of disease.
Linonophobia	–	Fear of string.
Teratophobia	–	Fear of monsters.
Phasmophobia	–	Fear of ghosts.
Oneirophobia	–	Fear of dreams.
Pteraphobia	–	Fear of flying.

Collectors and Collections

Arctophile	–	Teddy bears.
Bibliophile	–	Books.
Campanarian	–	Bells.
Cartophilist	–	Cigarette cards.
Cochlearist	–	Spoons.
Conchologist	–	Shells.
Deltiologist	–	Postcards.
Digitabulist	–	Thimbles.
Fromologist	–	Cheese labels.
Fusilatelist	–	Phonecards.
Grabatologist	–	Ties.
Lepidopterist	–	Butterflies/Moths.
Numismatist	–	Coins.
Philatelist	–	Stamps.
Phillumenist	–	Matchbox labels.
Tegestologist	–	Beer mats.
Vintitulist	–	Wine labels.

MISCELLANEOUS

Wedding Anniversaries

1	Paper.
2	Cotton.
3	Leather.
4	Linen/Fruit and Flower.
5	Wood.
6	Iron/Sugar.
7	Wool/Copper.
8	Bronze.
9	Willow/Pottery.
10	Tin/Aluminium.
11	Steel.
12	Silk.
13	Lace.
14	Ivory.
15	Crystal.
20	China.
25	Silver.
30	Pearl.
35	Coral/Jade.
40	Ruby.
45	Sapphire.
50	Gold.
55	Emerald.
60	Diamond.
70	Platinum.

Traditional Birthstones

January	–	Garnet.
February	–	Amethyst.
March	–	Aquamarine.
April	–	Diamond.
May	–	Emerald.
June	–	Crystal/Pearl.
July	–	Ruby.
August	–	Peridot.
September	–	Sapphire.
October	–	Opal.
November	–	Topaz.
December	–	Turquoise.

Signs of the Zodiac

	(Variable) Dates	
Aries	(Mar 21 – Apr 20)	The Ram.
Taurus	(Apr 21 – May 21)	The Bull.
Gemini	(May 22 – Jun 2l)	The Heavenly Twins.
Cancer	(Jun 22 – Jul 23)	The Crab.
Leo	(July 24 – Aug 23)	The Lion.
Virgo	(Aug 24 – Sep 23)	The Virgin or Maiden.
Libra	(Sep 24 – Oct 23)	The Scales.
Scorpio	(Oct 24 – Nov 22)	The Scorpion.
Sagittarius	(Nov 23 – Dec 22)	The Archer.
Capricorn	(Dec 23 – Jan 20)	The Goat.
Aquarius	(Jan 21 – Feb 19)	The Water Carrier.
Pisces	(Feb 20 – Mar 20)	The Fish.

NB. Zodiac actually means 'circle of animals'.
Libra (the scales) is the only non-living (inanimate) sign of the zodiac.
If you were born on or near one of the above dates, it is described as being born 'on the cusp', and you would have the characteristics of more than one sign.

The Greek Alphabet

α	–	Alpha	ι	–	Iota	ρ	–	Rho
β	–	Beta	κ	–	Kappa	σ	–	Sigma
γ	–	Gamma	λ	–	Lambda	τ	–	Tau
δ	–	Delta	μ	–	Mu	υ	–	Upsilon
ϵ	–	Epsilon	ν	–	Nu	φ	–	Phi
ζ	–	Zeta	ξ	–	Xi	χ	–	Chi
η	–	Eta	ο	–	Omicron	ψ	–	Psi
θ	–	Theta	π	–	Pi	ω	–	Omega

Note that the Greek alphabet has only 24 letters.

The Phonetic Code or Alphabet

A	Alpha	J	Juliet	S	Sierra
B	Bravo	K	Kilo	T	Tango
C	Charlie	L	Lima	U	Uniform
D	Delta	M	Mike	V	Victor
E	Echo	N	November	W	Whisky
F	Foxtrot	O	Oscar	X	X-ray
G	Golf	P	Papa	Y	Yankee
H	Hotel	Q	Quebec	Z	Zulu
I	India	R	Romeo		

Morse Code

A	dot dash	N	dash dot
B	dash dot dot dot	O	dash dash dash
C	dash dot dash dot	P	dot dash dash dot
D	dash dot dot	Q	dash dash dot dash
E	dot	R	dot dash dot
F	dot dot dash dot	S	dot dot dot
G	dash dash dot	T	dash
H	dot dot dot dot	U	dot dot dash
I	dot dot	V	dot dot dot dash
J	dot dash dash dash	W	dot dash dash
K	dash dot dash	X	dash dot dot dash
L	dot dash dot dot	Y	dash dot dash dash
M	dash dash	Z	dash dash dot dot

Heraldic Colours

Sable	–	Black.
Purpure	–	Purple.
Azure	–	Blue.
Bleu Celeste	–	Light blue, sky blue.
Murrey	–	Mulberry.
Sanguine	–	Blood-red.
Gules	–	Red.
Tenné	–	Orange, tawny.
Vert	–	Green.
Or	–	Gold (heraldic metal).
Argent	–	Silver (heraldic metal).

Order of Nobility or Peerage

Duke	–	Duchess.
Marquis, Marquess	–	Marchioness.
Earl	–	Countess.
Viscount	–	Viscountess.
Baron	–	Baroness.

Ranks of British Commissioned Officers

Royal Navy	*Army*	*Royal Air Force*
1. Admiral of the Fleet	1. Field Marshal	1. Marshal of the RAF
2. Admiral	2. General	2. Air Chief Marshal
3. Vice Admiral	3. Lieutenant General	3. Air Marshal
4. Rear Admiral	3. Major General	4. Air Vice Marshal
5. Commodore	5. Brigadier	5. Air Commodore
6. Captain	6. Colonel	6. Group Captain
7. Commander	7. Lieutenant Colonel	7. Wing Commander
8. Lieutenant Commander	8. Major	8. Squadron Leader
9. Lieutenant	9. Captain	9. Flight Lieutenant
10. Sub Lieutenant	10. Lieutenant	10. Flying Officer
11. Acting Sub Lieutenant	11. Second Lieutenant	11. Pilot Officer

Some World War II Codenames

Operation Dynamo	–	Evacuation of Allied Troops from Dunkirk (29th May - 4th June 1940).
Operation Sea Lion	–	Hitler's intended invasion of Britain.
Operation Barbarossa	–	Hitler's invasion of Russia (June 1941).
Operation Husky	–	Allied invasion of Sicily.
Operation Overlord	–	Allied D-day landings in Normandy (6th June 1944). *5 Normandy beaches:* Gold, Sword and Juno (British and Canadian troops). Omaha and Utah (American troops).

Prisons

Birmingham	–	Winson Green.
Dublin	–	Mountjoy.
Ford, West Sussex	–	Ford Open Prison.
Glasgow	–	Barlinnie (largest in Scotland).
Isle of Wight	–	Parkhurst/Albany/Camp Hill.
Leeds	–	Armley.
Lewes, East Sussex	–	Lewes Prison.
Liverpool	–	Liverpool (Walton).
London	–	Wormwood Scrubs (largest in Britain)/ Wandsworth (most prisoners in London)/ Pentonville/Brixton/ Holloway (women's prison).
Manchester	–	Manchester (formerly Strangeways).
Market Harborough, Leics.	–	Gartree.
Portsmouth	–	Kingston.
Princetown	–	Dartmoor.
Leavenworth, Kansas (oldest city in Kansas – 1854)	–	Leavenworth.
San Quentin, California	–	San Quentin (oldest prison in California – founded in 1852 and situated 10 miles from San Francisco).
Ossining, New York State	–	Sing Sing.

Former Prisons

London	–	The Clink (a prison in Southwark). The Marshalsea (a debtors' prison in Southwark until 1842). The Fleet (a debtors' prison near the Fleet river until 1842). Newgate (a famous prison last demolished in 1902-3 and now the site of the Central Criminal Court or Old Bailey).
Edinburgh	–	The Tolbooth.
Paris	–	Bastille (castle of St. Antoine – ancient fortress prison). Destroyed by the Revolutionaries after it was stormed on Tuesday 14th July 1789. Only 7 prisoners were found inside.
Alcatraz Island (San Francisco Bay)	–	Alcatraz (small island, name means 'Pelican', which was a federal penitentiary until 1963). Its inmates included 'Scarface' Al Capone, George (Machine-Gun) Kelly, and Robert Stroud, the 'Birdman of Alcatraz'.

Fictitious Prisons

Slade (television series *Porridge*).
Wentworth (television series *Prisoner: Cell Block H*).

World Airlines

British Airways/Virgin Atlantic	–	United Kingdom.
Aer Lingus	–	Ireland.
Delta/United Airlines/ Northwest Airlines/American Airlines/TWA	–	USA.
SN Brussels Airlines	–	Belgium.
KLM	–	Netherlands.
Iberia	–	Spain.
TAP	–	Portugal.
Alitalia	–	Italy.

Swiss	–	Switzerland.
SAS	–	Denmark, Norway, Sweden.
Finnair	–	Finland.
Lufthansa	–	Germany.
Olympic	–	Greece.
Aeroflot	–	Russia.
Lot	–	Poland.
JAT	–	Serbia.
Balkan	–	Bulgaria.
Tarom	–	Romania.
Malev	–	Hungary.
El Al	–	Israel.
Varig	–	Brazil.
Cathay Pacific	–	Hong Kong.
Qantas	–	Australia.

National Airports

Airport		*Serves*
Heathrow/Gatwick/Stansted	–	London.
Birmingham International	–	Birmingham.
Manchester International (formerly Ringway)	–	Manchester.
Liverpool John Lennon (formerly Speke)	–	Liverpool.
Woolsington	–	Newcastle.
Eastleigh	–	Southampton.
Lulsgate	–	Bristol.
Roborough	–	Plymouth.
Baginton	–	Coventry.
La Blaye	–	Alderney.
Ronaldsway	–	Isle of Man.
Squires Gate	–	Blackpool.
Edinburgh (Ingleston)	–	Edinburgh.
Prestwick	–	Ayr.
Dyce	–	Aberdeen.
Dalcross	–	Inverness.
Kirkwall	–	Orkneys.
Sumburgh	–	Shetlands.
Aldergrove	–	Belfast.

International Airports

Airport		*Serves*
JF Kennedy/La Guardia/Newark	–	New York.
Dulles International	–	Washington DC.
O'Hare/Midway	–	Chicago.
Logan International	–	Boston.
Stapleton International	–	Denver.
Hartsfield	–	Atlanta.
Lester B. Pearson	–	Toronto.
Dorval International/Mirabel	–	Montreal.
Uplands International	–	Ottawa.
Gander International	–	Newfoundland.
Charles de Gaulle/Orly	–	Paris.
Leonardo da Vinci	–	Rome.
Galileo Galilei	–	Pisa.
Marco Polo	–	Venice.
Barajas	–	Madrid.
North Front	–	Gibraltar.
Schiphol	–	Amsterdam.
Tegel/Schönefeld/Tempelhof	–	Berlin.
Kastrup	–	Copenhagen.
Cointrin	–	Geneva.
Kloten	–	Zürich.
Hellenikon	–	Athens.
Jan Smuts	–	Johannesburg.
Narita/Haneda	–	Tokyo.
Chep Lap Kok	–	Hong Kong.
KLIA	–	Kuala Lumpur.
Indira Gandhi International	–	New Delhi.
Dum Dum	–	Calcutta.
Ben Gurion	–	Tel Aviv.
Mount Pleasant	–	Falkland Islands.
Kingsford Smith	–	Sydney.

Main Railway Stations

Birmingham	–	New Street/Snow Hill.
Bristol	–	Temple Meads/Parkway.
Cardiff	–	Central/Queen Street.

Edinburgh	–	Waverley/Haymarket.
Exeter	–	Central/St. David's.
Glasgow	–	Central/Queen Street.
Liverpool	–	Lime Street.
London	–	Charing Cross/Euston/ Fenchurch Street/King's Cross/Liverpool Street/ London Bridge/Marylebone/ Paddington/St. Pancras/ Victoria/Waterloo.
Manchester	–	Piccadilly/Victoria.

International Car Registrations

A	–	Austria.	HR	–	Croatia.
AUS	–	Australia.	I	–	Italy.
B	–	Belgium.	IL	–	Israel.
BG	–	Bulgaria.	IRL	–	Ireland.
C	–	Cuba.	IS	–	Iceland.
CDN	–	Canada.	J	–	Japan.
CH	–	Switzerland.	JA	–	Jamaica.
CS	–	Czech Republic.	MA	–	Morocco.
D	–	Germany.	MC	–	Monaco.
DK	–	Denmark.	N	–	Norway.
DZ	–	Algeria.	NL	–	Netherlands.
E	–	Spain.	NZ	–	New Zealand.
EAK	–	Kenya.	P	–	Portugal.
F	–	France.	PE	–	Peru.
GB	–	Great Britain.	PL	–	Poland.
GBA	–	Alderney.	R	–	Romania.
GBG	–	Guernsey.	RA	–	Argentina.
GBJ	–	Jersey.	RC	–	China.
GBM	–	Isle of Man.	RUS	–	Russia.
GBZ	–	Gibraltar.	S	–	Sweden.
GR	–	Greece.	SF	–	Finland.
H	–	Hungary.	YV	–	Venezuela.
HKJ	–	Jordan.	ZA	–	South Africa.

FOOD AND DRINK

Varieties of Vegetables

Artichoke	–	Globe/Jerusalem/Chinese.
Asparagus	–	Connover's Colossal.
Bean (types)	–	Butter/Broad/French/Kidney/Runner.
Beetroot	–	Crimson Globe/Detroit Red.
Broccoli	–	Calabrese/Purple Sprouting.
Brussel Sprout	–	Citadel/Peer Gynt.
Cauliflower	–	Snowball/Majestic.
Garden Pea	–	Onward/Little Marvel.
Leek	–	Jupiter's Beard.
Lettuce	–	Iceberg/Paris White/Cos/Romaine.
Onion	–	White Silverskin/Best of All/Express Yellow/Scallion.
Potato	–	King Edward's/Maris Piper/Cara/Pentland Dell/ Homeguard/Désirée/Arran Pilot/Whites/Reds.
Radish	–	French Breakfast.
Turnip	–	Golden Ball/White Milan.

Varieties of Fruit

Apple	–	*Dessert*: Granny Smith/Cox's Orange Pippin/Costard/ Egremont Russet/Worcester Pearmain/Grenadier/ Golden Delicious/James Grieve/Beauty of Bath. *Cooking*: Bramley Seedling/Crawley Beauty/Newton Wonder/Irish Peach.
Cherry	–	Morello/May-Duke/White Hart/Stella/Florence/Emperor Francis.
Fig	–	Brown Turkey.
Gooseberry	–	Lancashire Lad/Lord Kitchener/White Lion.
Melon	–	Musk/Water/Honeydew/Cantaloupe/Galia/Ogen.
Olive	–	Calamata/Alfonso/Moroccan Oil.
Orange	–	Navel/Blood/Jaffa.
Peach	–	Duke of York/Rochester/Sea Eagle/Peregrine/Hale's Early.
Pear	–	Conference/(Doyenné du) Comice/William's (Bon Chrétien)/Bartlett.
Plum	–	Victoria/Czar/Mirabelle/Santa Rosa/Stanley.
Raspberry	–	Norfolk Giant/Lloyd George/Malling Jewel.
Strawberry	–	Red Gauntlet/Cambridge Vigour/Royal Sovereign/ Gento/Talisman/Pegasus/Temptation.
Tomato	–	Plum/Cherry/Beef.

Cheeses

English	Cheddar/Cheshire/Lancashire/Wensleydale/Double Gloucester/ Blue Stilton/Dorset Blue Vinny/Red Leicester/Red Windsor/ Sage Derby/Cornish Yarg.
Welsh	Caerphilly/Y Fenni.
Scottish	Dunlop/Craigrossie/Caboc.
French	Brie/Camembert (village in Normandy)/Roquefort (made from ewes' milk)/St. Paulin/Port Salut/Boursin/Morbier/Chaumes/ Reblochon/Pont l'Évêque/Chèvre/Bresse Bleu.
Swiss	Emmental/Gruyère/Appenzell.
Dutch	Edam/Gouda/Leyden.
Belgian	Limburger/Limoudou/Cassette.
Italian	Gorgonzola/Mozzarella (used in making pizzas)/ Parmesan (used with pasta)/Bel Paese/Ricotta.
Greek	Feta/Halloumi/Telemes/Pindos.
Norwegian	Jarlsberg/Gjetost/Ridder.
Danish	Danish Blue/Havarti/Svenbo/Fynbo/Samsoe.
Swedish	Greve.
German	Bayernland/Spitzkäse.
Spanish	Manchego/Roncal/Cabrales/San Simon/Mahón.
Polish	Tilsit.
American	Monterey Jack.

Wines

Region

French

Bordeaux	– Claret/Médoc (red)/Sauternes (sweet white).
Burgundy	– Mâcon (white and red)/Chablis (white)/ Bourgogne/Nuits St. Georges (red).
Beaujolais	– Beaujolais.
Champagne (around Reims and Épernay)	– Champagne.
Loire	– Muscadet (white)/Rosé d'Anjou.
Rhône	– Châteauneuf du Pape (red).

Italian

North East	– Soave (white)/Valpolicella (red).
Central West and South	– Frascati (white)/Chianti (red).

Central East	–	Lambrusco Bianco (white)/ Lambrusco Rosso (red).
German		
Mosel	–	Piesporter/Riesling (white).
Rheinhessen	–	Liebfraumilch/Niersteiner (white).
Portuguese	–	Vinho Verde/Madeira/Port.
Greek	–	Retsina.
Spanish	–	Rioja/Sherry.

Sizes of Wine Bottles (1 = Standard Size)

Magnum	2	Salmanazar	12
Jeroboam	4	Balthazar	16
Rehoboam	6	Nebuchadnezzar	20
Methuselah	8		

Cocktails (Main Ingredients)

Black Russian	–	Vodka, Kahlua (Tia Maria) and Coke.
Black Velvet	–	Guinness Stout and Champagne.
Bloody Mary	–	Vodka and Tomato Juice.
Bronx	–	Gin, Vermouth and Orange Juice.
Buck's Fizz	–	Champagne and Orange Juice.
Daiquiri	–	Rum and Lime Juice.
Harvey Wallbanger	–	Vodka, Orange Juice and Galliano.
Horses Neck	–	Brandy and Ginger Ale.
Manhattan	–	Whisky and Vermouth.
Margarita	–	Tequila, Triple Sec and Lime Juice.
Martini	–	Gin and Vermouth.
Piña Colada	–	Pineapple Juice, Rum and Coconut.
Pink Gin	–	Gin and Angostura Bitters.
Screwdriver	–	Vodka and Orange Juice.
Sidecar	–	Brandy, Cointreau and Lemon Juice.
Singapore Sling	–	Gin, Cherry Brandy and Lemon Juice.
Snowball	–	Advocaat and Lemonade.
Stinger	–	Brandy and Crème de Menthe.
Tom Collins	–	Gin and Lemon Juice.
White Russian	–	Vodka, White Crème de Cacao and Cream.

Zombie	–	Rum, Apricot Brandy and Pineapple Juice.

NB.

Gin and It	–	Gin and Italian Vermouth.
Rum and Black	–	Rum and Blackcurrant Juice.
Shandy	–	Beer and Ginger Beer or Lemonade.
Whisky Mac	–	Whisky and Ginger Wine.

Sauces

Which sauce is usually served with which roast meat:

Apple sauce	with pork.
Bread sauce	with chicken.
Cranberry sauce	with turkey.
Horseradish sauce	with beef.
Mint sauce	with lamb.
Orange sauce	with duck.

	Served with
Bolognese (meat sauce)	Pasta.
Napoletana (tomato sauce)	Pasta.
Tartare sauce	Fish.
Hollandaise sauce	Salmon.
Béarnaise sauce	Steak.

SPORT

Olympic Games Venues

1896	Athens.
1900	Paris.
1904	St. Louis, Missouri.
1908	London.
1912	Stockholm.
1920	Antwerp.
1924	Paris (film – *Chariots of Fire*).
1928	Amsterdam (women allowed to compete).
1932	Los Angeles.
1936	Berlin (Jesse Owens wins 4 gold medals).
1948	London.
1952	Helsinki.
1956	Melbourne.
1960	Rome.
1964	Tokyo (Judo introduced).
1968	Mexico (Bob Beamon's record long-jump).
1972	Munich (11 Israeli athletes massacred).
1976	Montreal (African boycott).
1980	Moscow (Western boycott).
1984	Los Angeles (Eastern bloc boycott).
1988	Seoul (South Korea).
1992	Barcelona.
1996	Atlanta.
2000	Sydney.
2004	Athens.
2008	Beijing.

Sports Trophies

FA Cup/European Cup/World Cup	–	Association Football.
The Ashes/Sheffield Shield	–	Cricket.
Ryder Cup/Walker Cup/Solheim Cup/ Curtis Cup/Dunhill Cup/Eisenhower Trophy	–	Golf.
Davis Cup/Federation Cup	–	Tennis.
Swaythling Cup/Corbillon Cup	–	Table Tennis.
Calcutta Cup/William Webb Ellis Cup	–	Rugby Union.
Americas Cup/Admirals Cup	–	Sailing.
Thomas Cup/Über Cup	–	Badminton.
Drysdale Cup	–	Squash.
Leonard Cup/Middleton Cup	–	Bowls.
Stanley Cup	–	Ice Hockey.

Association Football

English League Soccer

	Team	*Ground*	*Nickname*
1.	Arsenal	Highbury	The Gunners.
2.	Aston Villa	Villa Park	The Villans.
3.	Barnsley	Oakwell	The Tykes.
4.	Birmingham City	St. Andrews	The Blues.
5.	Blackburn Rovers	Ewood Park	The Blue and Whites.
6.	Blackpool	Bloomfield Road	The Seasiders.
7.	Bolton Wanderers	Reebok Stadium	The Trotters.
8.	Boston United	York Street Stadium	The Pilgrims.
9.	Bournemouth	Fitness First Stadium, Dean Court	The Cherries.
10.	Bradford City	Valley Parade	The Bantams.
11.	Brentford	Griffin Park	The Bees.
12.	Brighton and Hove Albion	Withdean Stadium	The Seagulls.
13.	Bristol City	Ashton Gate	The Robins.
14.	Bristol Rovers	Memorial Ground	The Pirates.
15.	Burnley	Turf Moor	The Clarets.
16.	Bury	Gigg Lane	The Shakers.
17.	Cambridge United	Abbey Stadium	The U's.
18.	Cardiff City	Ninian Park	The Bluebirds.
19.	Charlton Athletic	The Valley	The Addicks/Robins/ Valiants.
20.	Chelsea	Stamford Bridge	The Blues/Pensioners.
21.	Cheltenham Town	Whaddon Road	The Robins.
22.	Chester City	Deva Stadium	The Seals/Blues/City.
23.	Chesterfield	Saltergate	The Blues/Spireites.
24.	Colchester United	Layer Road	The U's.
25.	Coventry City	Highfield Road	The Sky Blues.
26.	Crewe Alexandra	Gresty Road	The Railwaymen.
27.	Crystal Palace	Selhurst Park	The Eagles/Glaziers.
28.	Darlington	Reynolds Arena	The Quakers.
29.	Derby County	Pride Park	The Rams.
30.	Doncaster Rovers	Belle Vue	The Rovers.
31.	Everton	Goodison Park	The Toffeemen/Blues.
32.	Fulham	Craven Cottage	The Cottagers.

33.	Gillingham	Priestfield Stadium	The Gills.
34.	Grimsby Town	Blundell Park	The Mariners.
35.	Hartlepool United	Victoria Ground	The Pool.
36.	Huddersfield Town	Alfred McAlpine Stadium	The Terriers.
37.	Hull City	Kingston Communications Stadium	The Tigers.
38.	Ipswich Town	Portman Road	The Town/Blues/ The Tractor Boys.
39.	Kidderminster Harriers	Aggborough	The Harriers.
40.	Leeds United	Elland Road	The Peacocks.
41.	Leicester City	The Walkers Stadium	The Foxes.
42.	Leyton Orient	Brisbane Road	The O's.
43.	Lincoln City	Sincil Bank	The (Red) Imps.
44.	Liverpool	Anfield	The Reds/Pool.
45.	Luton Town	Kenilworth Road	The Hatters.
46.	Macclesfield Town	Moss Rose	The Silkmen.
47.	Manchester City	The City of Manchester Stadium	The Citizens.
48.	Manchester United	Old Trafford	The Red Devils.
49.	Mansfield Town	Field Mill	The Stags.
50.	Middlesbrough	Riverside Stadium	The Boro.
51.	Millwall	The New Den	The Lions.
52.	Newcastle United	St. James' Park	The Magpies.
53.	Northampton Town	Sixfields Stadium	The Cobblers.
54.	Norwich City	Carrow Road	The Canaries.
55.	Nottingham Forest	City Ground	The Reds.
56.	Notts County	Meadow Lane	The Magpies.
57.	Oldham Athletic	Boundary Park	The Latics.
58.	Oxford United	The Kassam Stadium	The U's.
59.	Peterborough United	London Road	The Posh.
60.	Plymouth Argyle	Home Park	The Pilgrims.
61.	Portsmouth	Fratton Park	Pompey.
62.	Port Vale	Vale Park	The Valiants.
63.	Preston North End	Deepdale	The Lilywhites.
64.	Queen's Park Rangers	Loftus Road	Rangers.
65.	Reading	Madejski Stadium	The Royals/Biscuitmen.
66.	Rochdale	Spotland	The Dale.
67.	Rotherham United	Millmoor	The Merry Millers.
68.	Rushden and Diamonds	Nene Park	The Diamonds.

69.	Scunthorpe United	Glanford Park	The Iron.
70.	Sheffield United	Bramall Lane	The Blades.
71.	Sheffield Wednesday	Hillsborough	The Owls.
72.	Shrewsbury Town	Gay Meadow	The Town/Shrews.
73.	Southampton	St. Mary's Stadium	The Saints.
74.	Southend United	Roots Hall	The Shrimpers.
75.	Stockport County	Edgeley Park	County.
76.	Stoke City	Britannia Stadium	The Potters.
77.	Sunderland	Stadium of Light	The Black Cats.
78.	Swansea City	Vetch Field	The Swans.
79.	Swindon Town	County Ground	The Robins.
80.	Torquay United	Plainmoor	The Gulls.
81.	Tottenham Hotspur	White Hart Lane	The Spurs.
82.	Tranmere Rovers	Prenton Park	The Rovers.
83.	Walsall	Bescot Stadium	The Saddlers.
84.	Watford	Vicarage Road	The Hornets/Brewers.
85.	West Bromwich Albion	The Hawthorns	The Throstles/Albion/ The Baggies.
86.	West Ham United	Upton Park	The Hammers/Irons.
87.	Wigan Athletic	JJB Stadium, Robin Park	The Latics.
88.	Wimbledon	The Stadium, Milton Keynes	The Dons.
89.	Wolverhampton Wanderers	Molineux	The Wolves.
90.	Wrexham	Racecourse Ground	The Robins.
91.	Wycombe Wanderers	Causeway Stadium	The Blues/Chairboys.
92.	Yeovil Town	Huish Park	The Glovers.

Scottish League

1.	Aberdeen	Pittodrie (Stadium)	The Dons.
2.	Airdrie United	New Broomfield Park	The Diamonds.
3.	Albion Rovers	Cliftonhill Stadium	The Wee Rovers.
4.	Alloa Athletic	Recreation Park	The Wasps.
5.	Arbroath	Gayfield Park	The Red Lichties.
6.	Ayr United	Somerset Park	The Honest Men.
7.	Berwick Rangers	Shielfield Park	The Borderers.
8.	Brechin City	Glebe Park	City.
9.	Celtic	Celtic Park/Parkhead	The Bhoys.
10.	Clyde	Broadwood Stadium	The Bully Wee.

11.	Cowdenbeath	Central Park	Cowden/Blue Brazil.
12.	Dumbarton	Strathclyde Homes Stadium	The Sons.
13.	Dundee	Dens Park	The Dark Blues/Dee.
14.	Dundee United	Tannadice (Park)	The Terrors.
15.	Dunfermline Athletic	East End Park	The Pars.
16.	East Fife	Bayview Park	The Fifers.
17.	East Stirling	Firs Park	The Shire.
18.	Elgin City	Borough Briggs	Black and Whites.
19.	Falkirk	Brockville Park	The Bairns.
20.	Forfar Athletic	Station Park	The Loons/Sky Blues.
21.	Greenock Morton	Cappielow (Park)	The Ton.
22.	Gretna	Raydale Park	Black and Whites.
23.	Hamilton Academical	New Douglas Stadium	The Accies.
24.	Heart of Midlothian	Tynecastle (Park)	The Jam Tarts.
25.	Hibernian	Easter Road	The Hi-Bees.
26.	Inverness Caledonian Thistle	Caledonian Stadium, East Longman	Caley Thistle/The Jags.
27.	Kilmarnock	Rugby Park	The Killies.
28.	Livingston	Almondvale	Livi Lions.
29.	Montrose	Links Park	The Gable Endies.
30.	Motherwell	Fir Park	The Well.
31.	Partick Thistle	Firhill Stadium	The Jags.
32.	Peterhead	Balmoor	Blue Toon.
33.	Queen of the South	Palmerston Park	The Doonhamers/ Queens.
34.	Queen's Park	Hampden Park	The Spiders.
35.	Raith Rovers	Stark's Park	The Rovers.
36.	Rangers	Ibrox (Stadium)	The Blues/Gers.
37.	Ross County	Victoria Park	County.
38.	St. Johnstone	McDiarmid Park	The Saints.
39.	St. Mirren	Love Street	The Buddies.
40.	Stenhousemuir	Ochilview (Park)	The Warriors.
41.	Stirling Albion	Forthbank Stadium	The Albion.
42.	Stranraer	Stair Park	The Blues.

Cricket

County Grounds (+ Universities)

Derbyshire	Nottingham Road	Derby.
Durham	Riverside Ground	Chester-le-Street.

Essex	New Writtle Street	Chelmsford.
Glamorgan	Sophia Gardens	Cardiff.
Gloucestershire	Nevil Road	Bristol.
Hampshire	The Rose Bowl	West End.
Kent	St. Lawrence	Canterbury.
Lancashire	Old Trafford	Manchester.
Leicestershire	Grace Road	Leicester.
Middlesex	Lord's	London.
Northamptonshire	Wantage Road	Northampton.
Nottinghamshire	Trent Bridge	Nottingham.
Somerset	St. James's Street	Taunton.
Surrey	The Oval	London.
Sussex	Eaton Road	Hove.
Warwickshire	Edgbaston	Birmingham.
Worcestershire	New Road	Worcester.
Yorkshire	Headingley	Leeds.
Cambridge	Fenner's	Cambridge.
Oxford	The Parks	Oxford.

Rugby Union

The 6-Nations Championship – International Grounds

England	Twickenham	London.
Scotland	Murrayfield	Edinburgh.
Wales	Millennium Stadium	Cardiff.
Ireland	Lansdowne Road	Dublin.
France	Stade de France	Paris.
Italy	Flaminio Stadium	Rome.

Lawn Tennis

Grand Slam Events

Australian Open	Melbourne Park	Melbourne.
French Open	Stade Roland Garros	Paris.
All-England Championships	Wimbledon	London.
US Open	Flushing Meadow(s)	New York.

Golf

The 4 major Tournaments (Medal Play)

US Masters (Augusta, Georgia).	British Open.
US Open.	US PGA.

Matchplay

World Match Play – Wentworth.

Scoring System

Double Bogey	–	2 over Par.	Birdie	–	1 under Par.
Bogey	–	1 over Par.	Eagle	–	2 under Par.
Par	–	Expected number of strokes for a hole (or round).	Albatross (Double Eagle in USA)	–	3 under Par.

Snooker

World Professional Championship	–	Crucible Theatre, Sheffield.
British Open	–	Assembly Rooms, Derby.
UK Open	–	Guild Hall, Preston.
The Masters	–	Wembley Arena.

Points value of each ball

Red	–	1 point.	Blue	–	5 points.
Yellow	–	2 points.	Pink	–	6 points.
Green	–	3 points.	Black	–	7 points.
Brown	–	4 points.			

NB. The maximum break is 147.

Horse Racing

Flat Racing – The 5 English Classics

Derby/Oaks	–	Epsom.
1,000 Guineas/2,000 Guineas	–	Newmarket (home of the Jockey Club).
St. Leger	–	Doncaster.

Flat Racing – International Classic Races

Irish Sweeps Derby	–	The Curragh.
French Derby	–	Chantilly.
Prix de l'Arc de Triomphe	–	Longchamp.
Kentucky Derby	–	Churchill Downs.
Million Dollar Classic	–	Arlington.
Melbourne Cup	–	Flemington.

Hurdles and Steeplechases

Grand National	–	Aintree.
Scottish Grand National	–	Ayr.
Welsh Grand National	–	Chepstow.
Irish Grand National	–	Fairyhouse.
Gold Cup	–	Cheltenham.

Motor Racing

Formula One Grand Prix Races

Event		*Circuit/Venue*
Argentinian	–	Buenos Aires.
Australian	–	Melbourne.
Austrian	–	Zeltweg.
Bahrain	–	Bahrain International.
Belgian	–	Spa-Francorchamps.
Brazilian	–	Interlagos (São Paulo).
British	–	Silverstone (Northants)/ Donington Park (Leics.).
Canadian	–	Montreal.
French	–	Magny-Cours/Le Castellet.
German	–	Hockenheim/Nürburgring.
Hungarian	–	Hungaroring, Budapest.
Italian	–	Monza (near Milan).
Japanese	–	Suzuka/Aida.
Malaysian	–	Sepang, Kuala Lumpur.
Mexican	–	Mexico City.
Monaco	–	Monte Carlo.
Portuguese	–	Estoril.
San Marino	–	Imola (Italy).
South African	–	Kyalami.
Spanish	–	Barcelona/Jerez.

United States (North American)	–	Indianapolis/Phoenix/Detroit/ Los Angeles (Long Beach).

The Formula One Grand Prix season comprises 16 races. The points awarded to the top eight drivers in each race are: (1) 10 pts; (2) 8 pts; (3) 6 pts; (4) 5 pts; (5) 4 pts; (6) 3 pts; (7) 2 pts; (8) 1pt.

Number of Players in a Team

Polo	–	4	Cricket	–	11
Curling	–	4	(Field) Hockey	–	11
Basketball	–	5	Stoolball	–	11
Ice Hockey	–	6	Lacrosse	–	12
Volleyball	–	6	(10 Canada and USA)		
Netball	–	7	Shinty	–	12
Water-polo	–	7	Rugby League	–	13
Baseball	–	9	Rugby Union	–	15
Rounders	–	9	Gaelic Football	–	15
American Football	–	11	Hurling	–	15
(12 Canada)			Australian Rules	–	18
Association Football	–	11			(+ 2 reserves)

GAMES

Chess

It is generally believed that chess was first played in India around AD 570. The word 'checkmate' derives from the Persian *shah mat* meaning the 'king is dead'. The modern game including the 'castling' and *en passant* rules only became firmly established by the 18th century.

Relative Points Value of the Chessmen

Pawn (P)	–	1 point.	Rook or Castle (R)	–	5 points.
Knight (N or Kt)	–	3 points.	Queen (Q)	–	9 points.
Bishop (B)	–	3 points.			

The King (K) is not given a value as it is indispensable.

The front cover illustration is a detail from the painting by Leo Stevenson that is based on W. F. Yeames's *And When Did You Last See Your Father?*. It was painted to mark the end of the original form of *Mastermind* on BBC Television in 1997. The main inquisitor is Magnus Magnusson KBE, and it includes other people associated with the programme and the Mastermind Club, a club for all those who have been interrogated in the famous chair. Dramatis Personae are: left to right, the young girl as in the original; John Gilpin, the long-standing BBC studio floor manager for *Mastermind*; David Mitchell, the Producer and Director of *Mastermind*; the young boy as in the original; Peter W. J. Chitty, Mastermind Club Secretary; Christopher Hughes, the train-driving *Mastermind* Champion of 1983; Magnus Magnusson, KBE, Question master of *Mastermind*. Missing from the cover, but appearing in the original, are Leo Stevenson, artist and contestant; Christine L. Moorcroft, contestant; Dee Wallis, question-setter and organiser; Gerald Powell-Mackenzie, contestant; and Ray Ward, contestant.

This compendium of **General Knowledge** is aimed at helping to stimulate fact-based learning. The success of the many quiz shows on TV and radio, pub quizzes and fact-based games for adults and children, indicates a strong underlying interest everywhere. This wide-ranging collection of facts covers history, geography, literature, religion, mythology, mathematics, science, philosophy, psychology, the arts, film and sport. It will appeal to the whole family.

The Author has coached his school general knowledge team (The Prebendal School, Chichester) since 1981. During a nineteen-year period (1984-2003) the team reached the final of the Wessex (South of England) Region of the Junior (under 14) Schools Challenge Competition fifteen times, winning on eight occasions. Five of its victories led the team, via an inter-regional contest, to the UK national finals, culminating in the team being crowned UK National Champions in June 2000. On a more personal level, Stanley Prince has appeared on BBC's *Masterteam* and Channel 4's *15-1*, while the quiz league team he represented won the Championship of Chichester five years in succession (1990-94) and several other regional contests. In 1998 he established a new record by winning 18 successive editions of Channel 5's *100% Gold*.

Stanley Prince gained his degree in modern languages and philosophy, and his postgraduate certificate in education, in London, while studying for some time at the Universities of Bonn and Grenoble. His previous book is *A Guide to French Grammar* (also published by Packard Publishing Limited). He is an accomplished chess player and reached the level of playing two International Grand Masters, securing a draw against one of them. He is also a passionate theatre-goer, serving on the 1995-96 Laurence Olivier Awards Panel, and sees about 100 plays and shows a year, while retaining a similar enthusiasm for the cinema, art, music, sport and travel.